Age of Arousal

by Linda Griffiths

Wildly inspired by
George Gissing's *The Odd Women*

COACH HOUSE BOOKS

TORONTO

first edition

For production enquiries, please contact Michael Petrasek, Kensington Literary Representation, kensingtonlit@rogers.com or 416 979 0187.

Published with the assistance of the Canada Council for the Arts and the Ontario Arts Council. Coach House Books is also grateful for the support of the Government of Canada through the Book Publishing Industry Development Program.

LIBRARY AND ARCHIVES CANADA CATALOGUING IN PUBLICATION

Griffiths, Linda, date
    Age of arousal / Linda Griffiths.

A play.
ISBN 978-1-55245-190-8

    1. Suffrage–Great Britain–Drama. I. Title.

PS8563.R536A68 2007   C812'.54   C2007-907044-2

Dedicated to my mother,
Pauline Maclean Griffiths

CONTENTS

by Layne Coleman

I don't know anyone who works harder than Linda Griffiths at getting it right. I don't know anyone with her kind of will. I simply don't. I see Linda, sparking intelligence, hurling her head back and laughing, shrieking with delight about a friend of hers who posseses boundless energy, 'We should all be drinking her blood.' You could do a lot worse than to drink Linda's blood if you wanted to learn the art and craft of playwriting. It's a cliché to say the theatre is a demanding mistress, but it's true – it sucks your blood and spits you out confused and broken. And there's always more work to do. There's always another rewrite, another hill off in the distance.

Linda has managed her talent well. She has written eight full-length plays and four shorter works. Considering that a play may take from three to five years, this is quite an accomplishment. And Linda doesn't just bang them off. This woman worries them down to the bone. She does her homework and she does the tough slog. And the public loves her work, adores her – she's box-office gold. Sometimes I think Linda is embarassed by this, as if the public's affection were something to apologize for. Linda has achieved the kind of success in Canadian theatre that sets her apart. Linda's success did not come through luck or not suffering dark periods. It's a blessing that, when it's good, it's very very good. And it's never not good with Linda. Sometimes it's just more good than ever before. *Age of Arousal* is the best of the good. This is her finest wine, her deepest work, aged and honed and singing every breath along the path, every idea a challenge, an invitation to greatness. This play leads the audience inside the genius of Victorian women. Linda has chosen the Victorian age as the ship that will carry her richest cargo, and she has chosen well. This age is the one that Linda would be most comfortable in. But this is not a look back in time. This play is a cry to race towards the present.

Age of Arousal is a real feast of the theatre. You sit down, you enter another world, you lose yourself in another age – but inside it is an age remarkably like your own, an age when women have to fight for everything: dignity, love, equality. It is a fever dream, but you don't turn off your intelligence, you turn it on. The play is a set of Chinese boxes, opening one after another, each box leading to the next, each one lit with an inner fire of the glorious, suffering horror of sensuality, extraordinary intelligence and centuries of injustice, yet alive to the smells and thrills that life has to offer. Rattling and breaking their chains, these women in her play lift us into a domain we haven't inhabited before in Canadian theatre. These are Victorian tigers let loose in the mall, Victorian tigers who smack us upside the face with delight, with the force of their vitality and struggle. They can hurt you, but you're going on an unforgettable ride, one where you are going to be laughing hard with everyone in the theatre, and you will be moved. Moved by humanity and by the long march.

Layne Coleman, a former Artistic Director of Theatre Passe Muraille, continues to act in and direct Canadian plays while writing and living on a farm outside of Kingston.

In the late nineteenth and early twentieth centuries, women fought in confusion and clarity, wisely and stupidly, for liberation. The ideals were high and complex – they included a world view of what women and men could each offer society if only a balance between the sexes were allowed. They fought for equality but for more than equality – they fought, as Germaine Greer says, 'to allow our differences dignity and prestige.' These are my philosophical ancestors. I always wanted to know more about them but was too lazy to find out until seven years ago, when I found a battered paperback in a second-hand bookstore and bought it for a dollar. It was a little-known Victorian novel by George Gissing called *The Odd Women*. As I've worked on this play, which I knew would never be an 'adaptation', I've sometimes felt Gissing standing at my shoulder, staring at my screen, wondering what appalling liberties I was going to take with his book. I have taken liberties. I've taken his basic characters and situation and leapt off a cliff I was dying to leap off. I like to think that he would say, 'You go, girl.' But maybe not. Maybe he'll haunt me. I take the chance because the themes and characters of that age came bursting out of the keyboard, not as dry historical figures, but sexual and lubricious, explosive and contradictory. They beat down any idea of a buttoned-up age, they wept and fought, they made no sense, they made too much sense, they stretched my brain and encouraged the most delicious time travel. And so the dance of thievery and creativity has been danced with Gissing floating above, patron saint or appalled spectre.

WILDLY INSPIRED

George Gissing (1857–1903) lived only forty-seven years, but in that time he wrote twenty-three novels. Gissing's first books, published in the 1880s, were grimly realistic studies of life in London slums. His best-known is *New Grub Street*, about the financial and marital difficulties of a group of struggling authors. Some readers are repelled by his gloom, others find his subject matter courageous.

Most critics agree that his work offers unique insights into his time, including what it meant to be a not quite successful writer at the close of the nineteenth century. The details of his private life, which for much of his time was miserable, have fascinated readers for generations. He had two disastrous marriages, but at the end of his life some believe he finally found a happy relationship.

At first I read *The Odd Women* assiduously, using lots of coloured stickies. Just the way you would if you were writing an adaptation. Except Virginia went to Berlin. Mary became an ex-militant suffragette with guilt feelings over leaving the tough stuff. There were many turns away, but still the first draft was reasonably close to the novel. Months later I looked at the script and was totally bored. I was sick of subtext – the whole point of the Victorians was that there was so much underneath, but why should it be eternally underneath? I started thinking of a previous play, *The Darling Family*, where the subtext was so vital and in such contrast to the external text that it was spoken. I started to experiment with what I began to call thoughtspeak, and everything kicked into high gear. I dropped characters, altered characters, deleted threads of plot. The thing started galloping, and I could barely keep up. My own research on the women's suffrage movement and the Victorian age took precedence over the novel. I deliberately avoided the book, refusing to read it again. But the basis was all there and a few scenes are still fairly close to Gissing's. There is now a subtitle, 'Wildly Inspired by George Gissing's *The Odd Women*.' 'Wild,' not only because of the pace and style, but because of the liberties I took. 'Inspired,' because without Gissing's inspiration there would be no play.

But I knew I would have to be merciless with George Gissing. I would have to offend him and ignore him and make him squirm. I wanted to take the basic situation and basic characters and move them in my own direction without caring about George. But of course I did.

Dear George,

It's not that I don't care – I do. But I have taken your idea. I used your character names because I wanted that to be clear. They ask me how the play is different from the book and I want to say completely but that's not true. I know you had a hard life, that you married a prostitute, that you really tried to understand women, to break the class barrier, to be kind. But I have to say that there's a lot of what I would call misogyny in *The Odd Women,* even though the basic situation is so ahead of its time. Sometimes the things you have the characters say about women made me writhe. But in other places it is so powerful. Even Shaw never put that many women together in the same work. I found it dark, George. I know you saw many dark things and that your age was so filled with the contrast of light and dark. I added the element of sex and I don't think that's inappropriate, given your first marriage. You couldn't write about it, but I can. When I've felt you over my shoulder, I've never been able to tell if it was a benevolent presence. You reached and yearned, George, I know that. And now this woman has reached into what you did and has done what she wanted. There is a George Gissing Society and I'm afraid they'll want to tar and feather me. What you did is a flawed, brilliant thing – how bad is that? How bad am I to build on it? You found love in the end and I'm so glad. And people know your work and care about it even now. I'm one of them.

Love, Linda.

FABULISM AND REALITY

Age of Arousal's relationship to theatrical realism is something like its relationship to Gissing. A little dyslexic. Maybe dysfunctional. My theatrical style has always been hard to describe. At some point in every rehearsal I end up waving my arms, pacing up and down and blurting out, 'But it's not real!' This is usually an illuminating moment born of pain and irritation on all sides. I probably should say, 'But it's not naturalism,' but that doesn't seem to fit either. Finally I thought of calling myself a fabulist – without really knowing what it meant. I looked it up. It turned out that science-fiction writers were once called fabulists. Fantasy writers are fabulists too. I imagined fabulists sitting around Paris in the twenties, their minds filled with Rousseau's leaves, Freud's cigars, Grimm's fairy tales – also zeppelins, motor cars and telephones. The surrealists about to take off. But this was too fable. What about the turn of communism, of Hitler rising? I like to thread fantasy through a political eye. The problem with the fabulist definition is that the work is often inspired by something very specific, a person or an issue, often both. Then comes the unreal. Fantasists are escapists and so am I, but that's not the whole story. When I started my company, Duchess Productions, I tried to articulate a sense of this work.

Duchess Productions: Mandate

Duchess attempts to dance between the personal, the political and the fantastic.

Work about politics, illness, native/white relations, abortion, royalty and baseball does have a common thread. Duchess is called Duchess as a bit of fantasy, but also to evoke mythology and political absurdity.

Duchess is dedicated to a sense of the fantastic in theatre, both in terms of a celebration of language and theatrical image. It creates work that deals with the heightened word that is sometimes evolved through a combination of improvisational work and traditional methods of playwriting. The process of creation changes with each project. The goal is to create theatre that is highly literate, physically imaginative and emotionally connected. A theatre where an exploration of the surreal does not exclude a love of language. Add to this an awareness of the topical, of political or social issues explored without reverting to polemic. While Duchess learns from a minimalist school, its roots are fabulist and populist, bridging the audience gap between the avant-garde and the popular without compromising what has come to be known as *edge*.

Age of Arousal doesn't take place in historical reality but in a fabulist construct – an idea, a dream of Victorian England. It is stuffed with historical facts and modern/Victorian issues, but the world created is unreal. The leaping-off point is the thoughtspeak, which is a tangible way to reveal the unreality as well as an expressionistic excess. If you go too far toward the dream, you lose the politics. If you ignore the dream, the thoughtspeak won't work. Always there should be a tension between the genuine struggle of each character to evolve and the dance of fantasy as the play unfolds. Who knows what day it is, how many months have passed? You can track through this detail in the script and hopefully it will all add up, but it will never be key in how to approach the play.

PRODUCTION

PERFORMANCE STYLE

In discussions before the first production, the main questions were 'How big?', 'What is the style?', 'How big do you play it?' It was impossible to answer then and still is. The play is crammed with ideas, but that's not really what's going on. Each actor must struggle to find a visceral connection to those ideas. Brain and gut, mind and quim, must unite to find the level of performance. No idea, no fact, is separate from these characters' emotions. This translates into its own performance style. *Age of Arousal* is highly theatrical. On one hand, characters are bumping into each other on streets, fainting on cue, but on the other, real pain and sorrow are experienced. Navigating between these poles is like navigating all the other contradictions in this play. Lose the exuberance and you lose the vitality and essential weirdness of the piece, go too far into a performative style and you lose the genuine emotions that drive the characters. Caricature is to be avoided. These characters are real and must be played for real.

THOUGHTSPEAK AND PERFORMANCE

These characters speak their thoughts in wild uncensored outpourings. The invented term is 'thoughtspeak'. Italics indicate a character is speaking thoughts. The italicized thoughtspeak lines are interspersed through regular spoken dialogue. Sometimes dialogue overlaps. The slashes (/) indicate an overlap of voices. The next actor begins speaking at the slash and continues speaking over the previous actor.

Thoughtspeak is a verbal eruption from the depths of self. As if Freud were sitting to the side, demanding that the characters say everything. Naturally, they don't. They don't even say everything in thoughtspeak. But, with regularity, thoughts come to the surface, they are whispered, shouted, quickly tossed off – they happen in a breath. To the characters, mere dialogue is not enough to contain the enormity of their emotional/intellectual struggle with the world.

The challenge for actors is to find a way to play the difference between thoughtspeak and regular dialogue. An interior voice must be found which necessitates a change in pace and intensity – a double rhythm. The thoughtspeak is verbose and quick, it should spill out like diamonds from a velvet box. The overall pace must be dynamic. The mantra for the whole play is 'the text should be acted on the lines, not between the lines'. Pauses should be carefully considered.

Thoughtspeak sections are never asides to the audience – they're part of the scenes themselves. Sometimes they can even be spoken directly to the other actor, who holds the emotion and intention of the previous dialogue. Thoughtspeak can be played out but never to the audience.

On the page, thoughtspeak is the thing that will either get people excited or turn them off. It's different in performance. I hate to call it a device or a technique, since having characters expectorate their inner feelings has often been part of my work. In *Maggie & Pierre*, the Pierre Trudeau character bursts out with the unspoken at regular intervals, as does Maggie. In *The Darling Family*, I first used italics to annotate the difference between spoken dialogue and unspoken, inspired by Caryl Churchill. *The Darling Family* also included what I came to call arias, in which two characters speak thoughts in long sections of overlapping text. But in *Age of Arousal* I took the idea farther and with more characters. Throughout the process of development I fiercely maintained that thoughtspeak would not only work like crazy for the audience, but ultimately would be actor-friendly – even joyful to play. This theory was tested in rehearsals where an early stumble-through revealed a horrible cacophony – it was impossible to tell thoughtspeak from regular dialogue and everyone seemed to be screaming.

Director/dramaturge Karen Hines developed a vocabulary to help actors find their way through the scenes, to answer this fundamental question: when one person is in thoughtspeak mode, what are the other actors doing? She said, 'You have to give the other actor their privacy.' It was a perfect way to describe what happens when an actor is stuck onstage while another actor says things she/he can't hear. You can look away slightly, cross to a table, you can stare straight ahead. At times, and this will work, you can look directly at the other actor. Avoiding an overuse of business, thoughtspeak sections can be a good time to press a handkerchief to a damp forehead, run a hand absently along a thigh, adjust a shawl, look at papers ... or it might be a good time to remain utterly still and within the scene. You just have to give the other actor their privacy.

Hines believed that if the first time thoughtspeak is heard, it's absolutely clear to the audience what the characters are doing, then things could be loosened up later in the play, especially in the second act when there is more morphing between the dialogues. In 'The Dream', the absolute disconnectedness of each character from the other's thoughts was, and is, essential. This involves a meticulous attention to the moment of entry into thoughtspeak and the exit out of thoughtspeak. Vocal tone, intensity, pace, physical attitude. Getting in and getting out. The thoughtspeak was choreographed down to the flutter of an eyelash.

For the second production, director Maja Ardal did a great exercise. After three days of table work but no actual rehearsal, she had the actors act out the play on their feet, scripts in hand, pulling chairs or tables as needed. They just winged it. When the self-staging became dyslexically confusing, they stopped briefly and figured it out. It was wonderful to watch how at times the thoughtspeak blocked itself. Then a couple of actors would find themselves looking at each other during an intimate bit, know it was wrong and have to back away. Even in this wild trip through the play, actors were finding the double rhythm between the dialogue and the thoughtspeak. Eventually, the thoughtspeak was choreographed down to the flutter of an eyelash. All roads lead to the same necessity.

KINDS OF THOUGHTSPEAK

There is no specific rule as to when thoughtspeak is used and when it isn't. For a long time I thought there should be, but then I realized I was making it up and it could happen whenever I wanted. There are lots of occasions when, like any play, the subtext does drive scenes. And just to complicate things, not all thought-speak is the same. I've created different categories and names. There is 'fleeting thoughtspeak', which takes place inside a scene, interspersed through regular dialogue. This can be jagged bursts of a single line, three or four lines or a series of exchanges. An example is at the beginning of 'Budding Morsel'. There are 'arias and choruses', which are mostly in the middle and at the ends of scenes. These are clusters of thoughtspeak text with two or more voices often overlapping, like in the food section of 'Remingtons'. With 'synchronous thoughtspeak', the other character seems to hear what is being thought or echoes it. These are sprinkled throughout the play – Rhoda and Everard at the end of 'Impressionists'. 'Dialogue thoughtspeak' verges on spoken dialogue in that the other character responds even though the text is in italics. This happens most often in the second act where the division between what we came to call speakspeak and thoughtspeak begins to meld – Mary and Rhoda in 'Packing'. Everard's speech in 'Budding Morsel' is unusual in that one individual character has a large thoughtspeak section to himself within a scene.

SET

The philosophy of theatre as an empty space which is then filled is the best one to follow with *Age of Arousal*. With all its transitions, this play lends itself to simplicity in terms of set construction. To set up Mary's sitting room as a naturalistic space with walls, bookcases and stairs creates difficulties, as there are too many scenes take take place in other locations. The first production was on a thrust stage, so the set became the furniture. In the set changes, which were marvels of invention, furniture whirled on and off. To give a sense of modernity, the look was light as opposed to heavy Victorian – furniture was upholstered in very *au courant* shades of robin's-egg blue and brown. The flooring was espresso, as were the bases of the chaise, tables and chairs. The Remingtons were set on three small wooden tables, allowing us to use just one or two type machines in a scene. There was even a typewriter waltz-transition, with the characters twirling the machines to music. In the second production, there was a more minimal approach to the furniture, with basic pieces used for different functions. Mary's house is still the base for the drama, but there was minimal use of furniture and more multipurpose pieces. The typewriters are best on separate, movable tables – these can even be metal computer tables, bringing the concept of the modern to the furniture as well. Pillows thrown on the floor are useful, giving both a modern edge to Mary's house and allowing the characters a freer movement style than is traditional.

LIGHTS

In *Age of Arousal*, a lighting designer is freed of the need for a naturalistic source for light. A beam of light can appear from nowhere. The 'Impressionists' scene allows for a use of strong Monet-like pastels, but a projection in a twirling black and red graphic can indicate that the Impressionists weren't just pretty but also provocative. There are possibilities for lush greens in the park, dramatic specials on the Remingtons, white light in the gynecologist scene. The lighting can be both dramatic and enchanted.

TRANSITIONS

No matter how minimally or maximally this play is staged, transitions will be central. They can be included in the drama. Characters can continue to relate to each other as changes occur around them: looks, touches, surreal moments. In Calgary, Monica twirled alone in the middle of changing furniture. In Toronto, the play was performed on a proscenium stage, but in both productions there was a constant web of connections between characters in the shadows while scenes transitioned. The idea is never to stop the action.

COSTUMING *AROUSAL*

The costumes in *Age of Arousal* are the real set. They send out the visual code for the play. Initially, I imagined that a fashion designer would do the costumes until it became clear that theatre designers were a much better idea.

Go to the costume books and websites, look up 1885, and you can find in excruciating detail what colours were worn, how high the necks, how big the bustles, how tight the corsets. But we are in another realm here, and that must be communicated through the visuals. Unlike Shaw, Chekhov, or Strindberg, *Age of Arousal* is a contemporary play set in the past. How to remind the audience of this modernity without overly commenting or losing the sense of period?

It works best to keep the basic Victorian silhouette. The costumes can all fit close to the upper body, with skirts long but not heavy, with a hint of bustle achieved through scrunched and gathered cloth as opposed to the appalling bum-shelf that was sometimes worn. Then it's time to play, especially with necks and bosoms. Even if the books say they were buttoned to the eyeballs, expose throats and upper chests in order to express, especially with Mary and Rhoda, a consistent sensuality. Monica should be, of course, deliciously exposed. Any time a costume can have a more sensual feel, go for it, regardless of perfect period detail.

A powerful area to give a sense of both fantasy and modernity is in the use of colour. The historical Victorian palette is very dark, with colour accents in the gem tones. By just lightening the palette, introducing light and deep pastels, a whisper of modernity can be achieved. There are many ways to go: the modern can be insinuated through texture, colour, fabric, through ornament and embellishment. There is a Victorian futurist look that could be explored. Whatever the choices, a strict adherence to what was done is to be avoided. Designer Jen Darbellay used black lace trim on Mary's gown (in the daytime – horrors!) and there was often a sprinkling of sparkle on necks and hems. Generally, the characters can be more dressed up than in conventional period. Using shiny silk-like fabrics as opposed to heavy velvets can create an effect that is light and airy, a little fantastic, but still ... Victorian.

In *Age of Arousal*, there is a lot of movement from indoors to outdoors, from Mary's sitting room to the park and back again. In 'perfect period,' the ladies would don hats and jackets, but shawls can also be used to give a taste of the outdoors without resorting to intense outdoor paraphernalia. Putting on a shawl is a lovely, fluid gesture and allows for smooth transitions. Without jackets, bodies are more sensual, more exposed. Hats are not necessary, even if ladies did always wear them. Not wearing a hat can be a tiny touch of rebellion. But little cloth purses that dangle from wrists are almost a necessity. Little purses can hold handkerchiefs for business when thoughtspeak is taking place. Handkerchiefs are excellent for fainting, pre-fainting and almost fainting.

Mary

The world of the play is Mary's world. She sets a good table and loves her luxuries, especially clothes. This is a hip Victorian woman and she should be dressed as interestingly and as sensually as possible. Mary's arc in the play is not towards more sexuality but, in a way, towards less. At the beginning of the play, her nightgown should be open, showing shoulders, collarbones, décolletage. In the second act, she would be even more careful to look great, as she fights the battle of contradiction. She may do what many women do after a break-up: change her hair, buy a new dress.

Rhoda

Rhoda is tricky because she can appear severe, which might be translated to her dress unless we take into account she is in a lesbian relationship and, prior to the first scene, has had lots of fun. Of course, there will be a desire to take her in a more sensual direction as the play progresses, but it's important to remember that she is already a well-dressed woman when the play opens. It may be that she is more elegant and well tailored at the beginning of the play, but she should still indicate a sensuality that is bubbling beneath and has been partially satisfied with Mary.

Monica

Monica's dress is referred to as 'tarty' in 'Remingtons'. Imagine her, with her shopgirl's wages, going to the mall. But Monica is smart and knows how to shop well even if there's a little too much trim and way too much décolletage. This must be achieved while keeping her lusciously attractive – she never looks ridiculous. Monica can look like a piece of confectionary candy. In the second act she still shows too much bosom but the materials are more expensive and the total effect is towards elegance. She learns taste without ever losing her extreme sexuality.

Alice and Virginia

Alice and Virginia are initially the most conventional characters. They're not sexual or even sensual at the beginning of the play. Typically, they would be dressed in browns and greys, but it's also possible to give a sense of clothing that has faded and seen better days. Dulled pinks and blues can indicate that these women are not only living in genteel poverty but are immature in the ways of the world. Alice in faded blue. Virginia in faded pink. Their clothes may be mended, but the sisters are not paupers with obvious patches on their skirts – they are ladies who have one dress that just might pass for acceptable in the lamplight. Alice is more buttoned up than Virginia. Her arc moves towards the sensuality of chastity. However this is interpreted, she can look more put together as the play progresses. Virginia never achieves herself dressed as a woman. In the first act, she should look conventional and unremarkable. When she arrives back from Berlin, her man's suit can be ill fitting, as well as torn. In 'Infidelity', when she returns to women's dress under protest, she can look truly dowdy. But she should be wonderfully revealed in the last scene of the play: in 'The Garden,' Virginia should be dressed as a stylish man of the period.

Everard

As a wag who has travelled abroad, Everard is both fashionable and slightly ahead of his time. Keeping to the concept of opening up buttons and throats whenever possible, frock coats that are open to the waist are better than the closed variety sometimes worn in the period. Everard has certainly been to India – his waistcoats can be colourful with a hint of chinoiserie, and his dressing gown may speak of exotica. Everard should be dressed delightfully à la mode – his clothes are brilliantly fitted, beautifully textured.

In traditional Victorian costume drama, the corset is *de rigueur*. Its use can be adhered to with an almost religious zeal. But the use of corsets should at least be questioned. Even in terms of historical verisimilitude, New Women were questioning everything that kept them chained. They were aware that tight corsets were bad for their bodies. Mary and Rhoda would not be trussed tight, even if they wear corsets to allow their clothes to fit well. Actors can be given a choice as to whether or not they want to wear corsets. Some will feel it that it helps period movement, others that the corset constrains them too much. It is vital that the actors feel free enough to move in a slightly modern way. They should be able to sit on cushions on the floor, to bend, to reach, even to sprawl. This alone gives the clue that we are pushing the boundaries of Victorian perfection.

ACCENTS AND CLASS

I took my lead from Gissing. He was concerned with middle-class women. I'm a middle-class woman, albeit a bohemian one, so I stuck with the program. As a Canadian, I couldn't imagine coming up with faux cockney, although I may have been able to deal with working-class Yorkshire. I was also genuinely interested in the rise of the middle-class during this period and the new layers of society that were evolving. The aristocracy is not involved in this play and there are no maids or servants, even though Mary would certainly have help to run her house.

All the women in *Age of Arousal* come from the same general class, although their experiences give nuance to this broad category. All of the characters except Mary have experienced a reduction in circumstance. Alice and Virginia remember better times, when they lived with their father in a 'gentleman's' house – meaning the gentleman didn't work and lived on inherited income. Monica would have only a vague memory of this life and has been raised in a harder world. The money, wherever it came from, has dwindled down to the last generation, who traditionally then had to work. Rhoda, the sisters' childhood friend, would have been orphaned in very similar conditions, but is a couple of steps down the ladder financially. Mary also had very little cash, although the Barfoot family included people like Everard's father, who clearly had considerable income.

Mary may count as upper-middle class, and she certainly conducts herself with a sense of noblesse oblige. In terms of wealth, Everard grew up in the best situation, before his nefarious activities resulted in a reduced inheritance.

British accents need to be used with this language, although overly plummy sounds aren't appropriate. What is known as 'Received Pronunciation' or RP helps to generate a middle- to upper-middle-class sound. Mary's accent may be slightly different as she has experienced a commoner's prison and a range of classes as a result of her suffrage activities. Monica, although she comes from a genteel background, is a shopgirl and consorts with the less genteel. Rhoda has bettered herself through education. Virginia and Alice are isolated in a gentrified world of their own. Everard's travels have broadened any pseudo-aristocratic twangs he may have exhibited when younger. In all these cases, we're talking about subtleties, as opposed to Mary sounding cockney or Monica reflecting a London street accent.

True to the world of the middle and upper-middle classes, and true to the rising of this new age, money is more of a factor than class. All these characters have a basic education, then it's a question of what they did with it.

Everyone in this play on the brink of tumultuous change.

Age of Arousal premiered at the Alberta Theatre Projects' playRites Festival in Calgary, associate-produced by Duchess Productions, in February 2007.

Mary Barfoot: Dawn Greenhalgh
Rhoda Nunn: Irene Poole
Virginia Madden: Valerie Planche
Alice Madden: Elinor Holt
Monica Madden: Gemma James-Smith
Everard Barfoot: John Kirkpatrick

Director: Karen Hines
Dramaturge: Karen Hines
Set Design: Scott Reid
Costume Design: Jenifer Darbellay
Lighting Design: David Fraser
Composer/Sound Design: Richard McDowell
Production Dramaturge: Vicki Stroich
Associate Director: Linda Griffiths
Production Stage Manager: Dianne Goodman
Stage Manager: Rhonda Kambeitz
Assistant Stage Manager: Michael Howard
Junior Apprentice: Nicholas Blais

The play was presented by Nightwood Theatre in Toronto, development-produced by Duchess Productions, in November–December 2007 at the Factory Theatre.

Mary Barfoot: Clare Coulter
Rhoda Nunn: Sarah Dodd
Virginia Madden: Ellen-Ray Hennessy
Alice Madden: Maggie Huculak
Monica Madden: Gemma James-Smith
Everard Barfoot: Dylan Smith

Director: Maja Ardal
Dramaturge: Karen Hines
Set and Costume Design: Julia Tribe
Lighting Design: Kimberly Purtell
Music and Sound Design: Eric Woodley
Assistant Set and Costume Design: Gulay Cokgezen
Assistant Lighting: Cameron Davis
Assistant Director: Audrey Dwyer
Stage Manager: Stephanie Marrs
Apprentice Stage Manager: Stephanie Nakamura
Production Manager: Stefan Lenzi

The US premiere took place at the Wilma Theater, development-produced by Duchess Productions, in Philadelphia, December 5, 2007, to January 6, 2008.

Mary Barfoot: Mary Martello
Rhoda Nunn: Krista Hoeppner
Virginia Madden: Roxanne Wellington
Alice Madden: Monique Fowler
Monica Madden: Larisa Polonsky
Everard Barfoot: Eric Martin Brown

Director: Blanka Zizka
Dramaturge: Karen Hines
Set Designer: Matthew Saunders
Costume Design: Janus Stefanowicz
Lighting Design: Russell H. Champa
Sound Designer: Troy Herion
Production Dramaturge: Walter Bilderback
Stage Manager: Patreshettarlini Adams

AGE OF AROUSAL

SETTING: London, 1885. A time of enormous political, emotional and sexual change. People are bursting their corsets with unbridled desire. There are half a million more women than men living in England. The women's suffrage movement is fuelled by sheer numbers. Women demand rights. Those who protest are 'unsexed'. But the tide is too strong. Passions erupt and confusion reigns …

CHARACTERS

Mary Barfoot: Sixty years old – definitely not an *old lady*. Charismatic, egocentric, sexy. Enjoys young women's attention and admiration. An ex-militant suffragette who now runs a school for secretaries. Is in love with Rhoda.

Rhoda Nunn: Thirty-five years old. An orphan who has become a New Woman with a tendency to zeal. Loyal, idealistic, physically passionate – about to burst into flower. Mary's lover and a teacher at her school.

Virginia Madden: Forty years old. Anxious, agitated and hyperbolic. Impoverished ex-governess and alcoholic. Confused about her sexuality – secretly desires to dress as a man.

Alice Madden: Forty-six years old. Ex-governess and sister to Virginia. The take-charge older sister – deeply conservative, but full of inner passion. Chastity is more than comfortable for her.

Monica Madden: Twenty-one years old. Delectable younger sister to Alice and Virginia. Provocative and playful. Struggles with an intense natural sexuality which becomes a revolutionary perspective.

Everard Barfoot: Thirty-five years old. Sensual, confident, enticed by the New. Cousin to Mary Barfoot. Ex-doctor just beginning a life of leisure. Falls in love with Rhoda and the Woman Question.

ACT I

SCENE I: THE DREAM

Mary Barfoot's sitting room.
It's a large, lush room, modern yet Victorian.
Piles of paper litter a desk.
Cushions are scattered on the floor.

Mary is in her nightgown, hair down her back. Rhoda is dressed.
Mary sits on cushions, leaning against Rhoda's knees while
Rhoda brushes her hair.

MARY: Ohhh, that's fabulous.

RHODA: It's still so lovely and thick.

MARY: Still?

RHODA: Not 'still' but –

MARY: Yes, 'still.' I'm not balding. Some women do get very ... ohhh exquisite, there must be sensory attachments in the scalp area –

RHODA: You haven't dreamt of the hunger strikes in a long time.

MARY: Then the dream returns and 'unmans me.'

RHODA: Tell me.

MARY: You know everything –

RHODA: Not everything –

MARY: True ... you lie on your hard cot and hear them coming, keys rattle, the prison cell is open, two doctors and four wardresses, with the equipment –

RHODA: You appeal to the wardresses but they've been hardened beyond recognition –

MARY: That's when you start writhing, even before their filthy hands hold you down, then a / steel instrument –

RHODA: A steel instrument prises / pardon, I –

MARY: A steel clamp prises the jaws open as far as they can go, it breaks the teeth, gouges the lips, blood running / from –

RHODA: Buckets of blood –

MARY: Not buckets –

RHODA: Then the / feeding tube –

MARY: The feeding tube, smelling of the previous woman's vomit, rammed down your clamped-open mouth –

RHODA: Agony, the tube is too large, it rips the throat, tears the organs, the pain is excruciating –

MARY: They pour the food down, there is a moment's relief, then the stomach revolts, vomits up the food through the tube, truly suffocating now, choking, gagging, hands clawing the air for breath, writhing like an animal. What a stupid woman I am, you think. How appallingly foolish. You don't care about women's rights, you care only for your own suffering.

RHODA: I've always wondered why the food is vomited up. Is it the consistency of the tube that makes it so difficult?

MARY: The stomach has shrunk, they pour down a rancid porridge – no, I'll say no more. You love the gory bits too much. A very female attraction to suffering, I suspect.

RHODA: Nonsense.

MARY: The dream always reminds me of what a coward I was.

RHODA: I hate it when you say that. You were a political prisoner, you marched, planned actions, were beaten with clubs.

MARY: I was always terrified and finally I fled.

RHODA: Remember, I've seen every one of your scars. You were a warrior.

MARY: A 'suffragette.' Hateful term. It made us seem like dancing girls kicking our legs out of pique. We were suffragists demanding nothing less than a total transformation of the lives of women from cradle to grave.

RHODA: You deserve to rest after what you accomplished and continue to accomplish.

MARY: Lying on satin cushions with roast goose in my teeth while my sisters –

RHODA: You are not a coward.

MARY: The last time they shoved me out the prison door I could barely walk. There was no reception to meet me, no carriage, no cheers at the gates. I couldn't help thinking of the rich women who always had a carriage waiting, pillows for their arses, new dresses to complement their slim figures.

RHODA: You felt the gap between rich and poor within the struggle.

MARY: I had barfed and bled for the last time. I found I wanted money. I wanted it, I wanted women to have it. You don't know me.

RHODA: I do.

MARY: A weak warrior.

RHODA: An Amazon.

MARY: Laying down my sword to open a school for female secretaries.

RHODA: I only wish I had the same opportunity to prove myself.

MARY: Do you? I never realized.

RHODA: I worry about it at times –

MARY: You want to know how you'd react under fire?

RHODA: I worry that I would run away as soon as I was truly challenged.

MARY: Shall I torture you to find out? Use the dreaded clamp?

RHODA: You'd have to arrest me first.

MARY: I arrest you and demand bail for your release. I demand … a kiss.

They kiss.

Shall we leave this place of business and retire to my rare and sinister boudoir?

RHODA: Your boudoir is ever a garden of delights, but you are upset, I am restless, and the accounts have been piling up. Let's stay awake and do some sinister business.

MARY: Such a practical woman. Yes, a great pile of outstanding loans. Bella Royston still hasn't paid her fee – she can pay, she found a good placement.

RHODA: She still comes to the Wednesday meetings. Remember when she arrived wearing your old suffragette banner and tripped over it –

MARY: She gets up grandly, tramps on it again / rips it down the middle –

They laugh helplessly.

RHODA: That high-minded look / reeking with self-righteousness –

MARY: Supercilious look –

RHODA: (*laughing*) Slowly, proudly walking up the aisle –

MARY: (*laughing*) As if behind a funeral –

Pause.

You shiver.

RHODA: There's a draft.

MARY: You were up when I began dreaming. Reading?

RHODA: Just restless.

MARY: Restless.

RHODA: I started on the accounts.

MARY: You're so plain. I'm glad that you're plain.

RHODA: But I dress well.

MARY: I pay you well. Still cold?

RHODA: Not really. *What has happened? Has something happened? Suddenly I want to crawl into the safety of her belly –*

MARY: *She's going to leave me, perhaps not, yes she will, she doesn't know but I know –*

RHODA: *Press the folds of her skin to my lips –*

MARY: *I'm on the brink of old age, all my flirting done / oh lord what a fate –*

RHODA: *What has happened?*

MARY: *Do not pack a bag in the middle of the night, do not tell me in a mature and confiding womanly way / that would send me to the grave –*

RHODA: *The force of her intellect gushing through mind and body, saving me from poverty, blindness, mediocrity –*

MARY: *I've filled her head, done nefarious acts to her body –*

RHODA: *Too timid to find my own body till she opened its secrets.*

MARY: *The icy breath of change.*

RHODA: *Nothing has changed.*

MARY: *Don't hate me when it's done.* I'm going back to bed. Are you coming?

RHODA: I'll just finish this note to Bella.

MARY: Don't be too long.

Mary exits.

SCENE 2: THE BUMP

A London street outside Victoria Station.
Virginia is drunk. Rhoda is not.
Virginia and Rhoda smack loudly into each other.
Virginia lands heavily on the ground.

RHODA: Ughhhh!

VIRGINIA: Ahhh!

RHODA: I beg your pardon!

VIRGINIA: I've been hit by a train, a horse, a great black steed, my limbs / are severed, my arm is falling off –

RHODA: No, not a train, a person, we bumped into each other, are you hurt / let me help you up –

VIRGINIA: Not hurt, not hurt –

RHODA: Virginia? Virginia Madden? It's Rhoda Nunn.

VIRGINIA: Nunn?

RHODA: Rhoda. We knew each other as girls.

VIRGINIA: Rhoda Nunn. Of course. You argued with my father about Parliament –

RHODA: How are your sisters?

VIRGINIA: Two are dead.

RHODA: My condolences –

VIRGINIA: There's only Alice and pretty Monica left –

RHODA: So many tragedies.

VIRGINIA: Ohh, dizzy …

RHODA: There's a tea shop just around the corner –

VIRGINIA: Tea shop? You think I can afford tea shops on five pence a day? Ohh, faint –

RHODA: Let me help you. Where do you live?

VIRGINIA: When Father died the whole world became a jungle, he was the lion and now there is nothing / but weeping spinsters as far as the eye can see …

RHODA: Put your arm over my … not that way … no, no, turn toward me – Virginia? Do you feel my arm?

VIRGINIA: Arm.

RHODA: Do you feel its strength?

VIRGINIA: Lovely. Yes.

RHODA: Then lean into me and I will take you home.

SCENE 3: BEDSIT

Three chairs represent a barren bedsit.
Alice has a bad cold.
Virginia and Rhoda enter.

ALICE: Achoo!

VIRGINIA: Alice! Look who I met on the street –

ALICE: Virginia! Where were you? I woke up from a nap and you were gone –

VIRGINIA: Alice, look / It's Rhoda Nunn, she was passing by –

ALICE: You cannot go wandering about by yourself, what would father have said? Rhoda who?

VIRGINIA: Rhoda Nunn!

ALICE: How could you have brought a guest / a guest! Rhoda who?

RHODA: Alice, we knew / each other as girls –

VIRGINIA: I was taken ill and she put out / her strong arm and –

RHODA: I have no intention of bothering you / but your sister –

ALICE: Ill? Are you ill? Do we need a doctor?

VIRGINIA: I am better now. It's Rhoda –

ALICE: Of course, Rhoda Nunn, from a happier time, forgive me, forgive my illness, forgive this room. We must sit down. We must be pleasant and civil. A visit. How gay.

RHODA: Perhaps we should visit at some other time –

ALICE: Pray be seated. Virginia, you are ill, lie down. I am in my nightdress.

VIRGINIA: Shall we have tea?

ALICE: Tea? Are you insane?

VIRGINIA: There must be some leaves left –

ALICE: No tea.

RHODA: I wrote when your father passed away but then moved house and –

ALICE: You were our poor little orphaned friend.

RHODA: Orphaned and poor? Yes, I suppose I was.

ALICE: Father, who was the whole world to us, where is his protection, oh God, his protection.

VIRGINIA: She looks pink-cheeked and prospective. Parsimonious?

ALICE: Prosperous.

RHODA: I have been fortunate. And … you?

ALICE: Father died. Then sister Martha died.

VIRGINIA: Sister Isabel expired horribly in the madhouse.

ALICE: Our guardian, Mr. Humelford, died of the putrid fever.

VIRGINIA: The house was sold, all our belongings sold.

ALICE: There is nothing left. We have recently lost our positions and presently are at leisure –

VIRGINIA: We did work. Have you ever been a governess? Five children looked after for room and board, not a penny of salary, and then they all went to Paris without me. They want certificates now. Formal education. The children were so much larger than I was, even the baby. Very very large.

RHODA: (*dizzily*) I must go.

ALICE: You will not.

VIRGINIA: Now Rhoda is looking faint.

RHODA: I am not given to fainting – *run from the cloying air, the genteel starvation, the stink of lavender, sweat and something else, something with yeast –*

ALICE: *She was a priggish girl even then, as if she were above us, as if she was going to get away, I'd like to smack her in the puss.*

RHODA: *But for a few bits of luck I could be them – I feel the sisters pulling at me, trying to drag me down, don't you dare, I've come too far, too hard –*

VIRGINIA: *I can smell the meat on her, mighty hunks of beef, grizzling platters of lamb –*

ALICE: We are not destitute, however it may appear. When our father died he left us eight hundred pounds.

RHODA: Eight hundred pounds? Not riches, but a fair sum.

ALICE: To be divided among five sisters. Three left. None married.

RHODA: Three? Of course, there was a little girl.

VIRGINIA: Our dear little Monica.

ALICE: Six pence a day for food. Fourteen shillings and tuppence a week. Two pounds, sixteen shillings and eight pence a month for three months and then … and then …

RHODA: Eight hundred pounds could be invested in any number of enterprises.

ALICE: We were advised by the guardian our father appointed never to touch the / principal.

VIRGINIA: Never touch the principal.

ALICE: It is our only security, the only bit of ground we stand on –

VIRGINIA: When we grow old and useless –

ALICE: When no one will give us even board and lodging for our services –

VIRGINIA: Then the principal will be all that keeps us from –

ALICE: The workhouse.

VIRGINIA: The workhouse.

RHODA: Women must stop leaving money matters to male guardians and protectors.

VIRGINIA: Father always said that no woman, old or young, should ever have to think about money.

ALICE: Monica is employed in a shop. They work her half to death, but she is pretty and she will marry.

VIRGINIA: Monica is pretty, Monica will marry.

RHODA: (*standing*) But how? How will she marry? Is it possible you aren't aware of it? For the first time in recorded memory there is an imbalance in the population of such enormity that it must be a sign from God, if you believe in God. Half a million more women than men in this land. Some say a curse, we say a miracle. The greatest opportunity has been given to us, as though someone were saying, 'I take away your props, your supports, your income, ay your slavery and degradation. You cannot marry, you cannot have children, you must rise up – you must be odd!'

Pause.

VIRGINIA: Is that chair uncomfortable? Try this one. I will move here, and you can move there.

ALICE: Too hard a chair. She needs a pillow, would you like a pillow?

VIRGINIA: She should have a pillow.

ALICE: Not that pillow.

VIRGINIA: It's the only pillow unless we use the bed pillow.

ALICE: We cannot use the bed pillow.

RHODA: No pillow! Forgive me. I've been told that I'm something of a zealot – get red in the face when I get going.

ALICE: Nothing of the kind – *very red.*

VIRGINIA: *So pleasantly red.*

ALICE: 'Odd,' as in …?

RHODA: Women who will never be paired.

ALICE: Oh. You're not married?

RHODA: I am not.

VIRGINIA: You sound proud of it.

RHODA: I am.

VIRGINIA: You support yourself?

RHODA: I work for a woman of independent means. My employer and I run a school for odd women, meaning –

ALICE: Your employer is a woman?

RHODA: Women must come to grips with two things in this age. Loneliness and money. I must go. I invite you to visit my employer, Miss Mary Barfoot. She's a remarkable woman who may able to assist you.

ALICE: Well, we / might …

RHODA: Good, it's settled. And please bring Monica. Sunday next?

VIRGINIA: Ah …

RHODA: Good –

ALICE: Then you are odd, Miss Nunn?

RHODA: Ferociously odd. Good day.

Rhoda exits.

ALICE: *Something is changing, a tonic that makes the eyes burn, like mountain air, too cold too bright –*

VIRGINIA: *As if a tonic had been administered. So thrilled, my breath is panting, every nerve springs forward at attention, a burning sensation throughout my limbs, a barking sensation in my mouth* – She is like a man –

ALICE: Prosperous.

VIRGINIA: And like a man. Resolving –

ALICE: Acting, planning, ordering people about.

VIRGINIA: We'll go for Monica.

ALICE: For Monica.

SCENE 4: BUDDING MORSEL

Sunday in a city park.
Bright sunshine,
ducks in a pond,
Everard and Monica walk together.

MONICA: This is my one free day. I often come to the park to enjoy the sun. You must know that I never go out with gentlemen I don't know. But as I am not acquainted with any gentlemen, my sisters know none, there are none in the streets, none in the shops …

EVERARD: So if you are to have any male company at all, you must take a risk.

MONICA: You seem safe.

EVERARD: *As safe as I can be around a budding young morsel.*

MONICA: *Be contained and virtuous, do not allow the flutterings down below – the fit of his fine wool trousers stretched over well-nourished thighs – no stop –* I work in a shop.

EVERARD: How lovely.

MONICA: I am endlessly in between – caught, you see. My sisters made me half a lady and half a shopgirl. *I want to lie with him while he licks fine wine off my belly, no, can't stop thinking about it, always thinking about it –*

EVERARD: What a delightful little metamorpho you are. I should put you on exhibit, 'Ladies and Gentlemen, here you see a hermaphroditus, half lady! Half shopgirl!' *And probably a virgin, about to be initiated / by someone –*

MONICA: *My eyes drop, of course they drop, to his marriage finger, that singular finger –*

EVERARD: *Ripe, needing to be plucked, breasts like / great round apples –*

MONICA: *And there is no ring –*

EVERARD: *Let me suck the cranberries of your nipples / suck the juice –*

MONICA: *Handsome, educated, a waistcoat that would cost / me a year's wages –*

EVERARD: *Let it dribble down my chin onto your tight little …*

MONICA: *Is he crippled in mind or body / has he detestable vices?*

EVERARD: *Teach you mysteries –*

MONICA: *No ring on his finger, no ring –* You're not married?

EVERARD: I can't afford to be married.

MONICA: But you're rich.

EVERARD: I'm not. I did work.

MONICA: But now you don't?

EVERARD: Now I'm a man of leisure with a small inheritance.

MONICA: *Monica is pretty, Monica must marry.*

EVERARD: Meet me here next Sunday. I want to see the sunlight glitter on your throat, I want to hear you prattle.

MONICA: My sisters are withered old maids. The sight of them makes me want to off myself. I'm bad, aren't I?

EVERARD: I too saw my family and thought, 'I will never be like them,' and so I became nothing. *She'll come next Sunday, I see it in her eyes.*

MONICA: *I've been immodest, I've been desperate.* I am so weary.

EVERARD: Yes, I believe you are. *I am striving to be a good man, yet a virile man, to search for my happiness without hurting others, to take pleasure in women because not to do so is to repress one of life's great joys, and so I do dally but often do not taste, I am not at the mercy of my staff, I have practiced the breathing methods of India to control my urges – yet when I see a woman of a certain shape, a certain smell, all the husbands I know are in a state of abject misery, this bargain is impossible to make, and yet I see a woman at my hearth, no not a hearth, in Venice, in Paris, a salon with a woman presiding, giving as good as she gets – could this odd girl become a real woman, a New Woman? I want to embrace my age, the machines and the women, I want to measure and to annotate, perhaps I might even work again if a woman were there to do what they do, to encourage and support, I would let her be free, I am no barbarian to lock a woman up, forbid her to walk alone, yet we would walk together.* Next Sunday then?

MONICA: Perhaps.

Mary Barfoot's sitting room.
Virginia, Alice and Monica arrive.
Mary and Rhoda receive them.

ALICE: Our deepest apologies, we are so / behind our time, we had to dress, of course, but then Virginia –

VIRGINIA: Such difficulties, Miss Barfoot, we were quite lost, the streets seemed to alter themselves / as we walked –

MONICA: It's a splendid house, real velvet curtains … ohhh, lovely touch –

MARY: And you must be pretty Monica –

VIRGINIA: *Does she look a little tarty? She does, she looks a little tarty.*

ALICE: *It is her chance, all our chances, hold fast, smile, dear girl, no don't smile, be serious, but not excessively serious –* They work her half to death for a pittance in that shop, Miss Barfoot.

MARY: Mary.

ALICE: Mary.

VIRGINIA: Thirteen hours on her feet, six days of a week.

MARY: Monica, do you wish to change your situation?

MONICA: No, I wish to sludge away in the dung heap of reputable slavery till I die a joyless old maid. Oh, forgive me, I didn't mean to, sisters, you know I love you, am grateful to you –

ALICE: I prefer 'spinster' to 'old maid.' 'Spinster' has dignity. A word from seventeenth-century France. A woman who spins fibre into thread at a spinning wheel, a woman who earns her keep.

VIRGINIA: We don't want Monica to end up like us.

MARY: No one has ended up anywhere.

MONICA: Is it true you were a suffragette? Did you starve yourself, were you beaten? *Flirting, can't stop, can't stop flirting, my body does it all by itself –*

MARY: *Fascinating, one of those girls who exudes sex scents from the cradle –*

MONICA: Have you heard the music hall song, (*speaking*) 'She's not a lady, she's a la di da for the vote'?

MARY: (*singing*) 'She won't have a sweetheart, she won't have a child or a coat, she'll only have a la di da vote!'

MONICA: Are all the women you teach spinsters?

ALICE: / Monica!

RHODA: Odd women.

MONICA: *Oh God, don't let it happen to me, alone alone, dry as a bone, wrinkled and hopeless and poor, never kissed, never lain with –*

RHODA: Odd or 'redundant' women. We prefer to be odd.

VIRGINIA: I feel redundant.

ALICE: I have heard that 'odd woman' means abnormal. A deviant / person –

RHODA: It is a privilege to be an odd woman.

MARY: It is as if the birth rate is on the side of women's rights. There are over four hundred thousand more women than men in this land. A flood, a torrent, a statistical bomb of women.

ALICE: Yes, Rhoda did mention the / population imbalance.

RHODA: Men downed by wars and sex disease, by drink and drug, women eating their vegetables, staying at home –

MARY: Female molecules forming together, ovaries creating more ovaries, wombs more wombs –

VIRGINIA: We did hear / from Rhoda that there is –

RHODA: One out of four women will never be able to marry. Without the burden of children and a husband, they have the leisure to contemplate their circumstances and the need to enter forbidden areas of employment.

ALICE: *We should never have come, our mended skirts, boots with holes, stomachs empty, let us lie down and expire on the carpet.*

MARY: Rhoda, dear, see to luncheon.

RHODA: Yes, Mary.

Rhoda exits.

MONICA: You are against marriage, then?

VIRGINIA: Of course she's not.

ALICE: Monica, you are too bold.

MARY: We are not against marriage. However, every happily unmarried woman is a silent reproach to the conditions of marriage. In this contract, a woman sells herself for her livelihood. She becomes the legal property of her husband, relinquishing all power over her wealth, her children and her own body. It is legal prostitution. The woman becomes an unpaid breeding machine, with fewer rights than any spinster in this room.

Mini pause.

VIRGINIA: Miss Barfoot, have you ever flung a bomb or offered a bomb, or however it's said –

ALICE: It is 'flung,' I believe. Yes, you must have many humorous stories of your exploits as a suffragette.

MONICA: Then you are against marriage.

MARY: Not in its essence. There are many married women in the movement, others are attempting free unions –

MONICA: Free unions?

VIRGINIA: Offering or flinging bombs and such –

MARY: My militancy was limited. I merely committed arson, window smashing and flooded men's putting greens with a thousand signs saying, 'No Vote. No Golf.'

Rhoda re-enters.

RHODA: Luncheon is ready.

MARY: I ordered a substantial meal, I hope it's not too heavy for you.

RHODA: We'll do this in the new style, as a buffet. Each person serves themselves.

VIRGINIA: Meat?

ALICE: Virginia became a vegetarian when she lost her employment.

VIRGINIA: But perhaps today, in honour of our hostess –

ALICE: Monica, make certain you eat. I am not very hungry, but perhaps a small selection –

Virginia, Alice and Monica begin to load their plates and eat during the rest of the scene.

VIRGINIA: *Goose stuffed with candied ginger, beef tongue with pear dressing –*

ALICE: *Capon with sliced oranges, roast Wellington with chives, I want to tear the flesh with my hands –*

MONICA: *Great plates of steaming oysters / slippery with butter, pimento, sprinkled with parmesan – hungry, so hungry –*

VIRGINIA: *Curried chicken with raisins and pistachios / so hungry hungry –*

ALICE: *Sweet vinegar and / beetroot, sage and watercress, ohh blessed saliva, hungry so hungry hungry –*

VIRGINIA: *Brandy, brandy in the plum sauce, brandy on the pears / brandy in the custard, lick the brandy, lick it up –*

MONICA: *Roast potatoes with rosemary, creamed parsnips / with parsley and salt –*

ALICE: *Delicious little carrots sprinkled with / cinnamon, nutmeg –*

VIRGINIA: *Sweet strawberries, chocolate rosettes, marzipan hearts –*

ALICE: *Turkish delight –*

MONICA: *This is a trap, it's in all the penny stories, the women ply you with food but it's filled with drug and when you wake, they ravish you.*

RHODA: Have you given any thought to your plans for the future?

ALICE: (*eating*) Plans?

VIRGINIA: (*eating*) Future?

MONICA: (*eating*) I'm getting married.

ALICE: Monica!

MONICA: In the future.

ALICE: Oh, yes –

MARY: But until then –

VIRGINIA: Our father brought us up to be ladies. Teaching, governessing –

RHODA: Starving.

MARY: Rhoda.

Rhoda and Mary draw apart.
Monica, Virginia and Alice continue eating.

RHODA: I can't bear these moping, mawkish creatures, and now this cheap miss –

MARY: Who must be protected. Why do you balk at these sisters? You've helped women like this all over London –

RHODA: I shouldn't have invited them. Suddenly I hate them –

MARY: Then you hate women, then our struggle is for nothing.

RHODA: So sick of prompting and praising, only to have them put the shackles back on their own wrists.

MARY: Oh, don't be so daft.

Mary addresses the room.

Rhoda and I will now give a demonstration of our secret weapon in the battle for equal opportunity.

Magical sound cue. Mary draws aside a curtain and reveals three Remington type machines, circa 1885, splendidly lit.

Behold the Remingtons!

ALICE: Remingtons! I have heard of them.

MONICA: Machines for the future –

VIRGINIA: Glorious, yet appalling. When I look at them I feel I am disappearing into thin air. Where is the beauty of the hand-written note which tells so much? The handwritten note is personal, physical, of the body, of mortal flesh –

ALICE: Virginia. You are not quite yourself.

VIRGINIA: It must be the meat. I murdered that beef.

MARY: And, to show off, yes women may show off, we will perform blindfolded. Alice, may I have your scarf?

Mary and Rhoda sit behind the Remingtons, blindfold themselves and begin to type like virtuoso pianists. What follows is a thrilling percussive duet played on the typewriter keys. The rhythms are complex and gutsy, reminiscent of tap dancing. They build to a crescendo. Rhoda and Mary end with a flourish and remove their blindfolds, amid clapping.

VIRGINIA: Thrilling! Spellbinding!

MONICA: A perfectly printed page –

ALICE: And this is what you teach?

MARY: We teach typewriting, shorthand, bookkeeping and correspondence.

VIRGINIA: Oh, I could never to do that.

RHODA: Which?

VIRGINIA: Any of it.

RHODA: Why not?

MARY: We enter the closed monolith of business humbly, as assistants and secretaries. But once our pointed boot is in the door, we may involve ourselves in commerce, investment, trade –

VIRGINIA: And you would accept us? The three of us?

RHODA: Well, we would need to discuss / all aspects –

MARY: Yes, we'll accept you.

ALICE: How lovely, so you help needy women.

MARY: No, this is a business, not a charity. Those who can't afford tuition take a loan, which is paid off when they find employment.

MONICA: And if they don't?

RHODA: They're indentured for life, like white slaves.

ALICE: We would live here?

MARY: There are rooms available, at an extra cost.

MONICA: You would own us.

RHODA: We would teach you.

ALICE: But men are secretaries.

MONICA: I've heard wives don't want female secretaries about,
tempting their husbands –

RHODA: The girls we teach can be around a man without jump-
ing into his lap over dictation.

MARY: Well, most of them can.

VIRGINIA: I don't know, I don't know – Alice?

RHODA: You may wish to think it over.

ALICE: No. *I want to plant a garden, I want to chance death by child-
birth, I want to manage my own home, scrub till my hands crack,
I want to shop for food, service a husband, whisper with women
about my genitals, I want to burn and sweat through the change
of life in quiet seclusion and yet I am denied, I am denied –*
Your offer is very kind. We accept. We will be enormously in
your debt.

MARY: I imagine a world where we might rage and cry, give birth,
weep for a kitten, then oversee a transaction worth millions.

MONICA: *Too many women, they'll pollute my thoughts, make me ashamed of my desires, I have to find a man, a hundred men, before it happens to me –*

RHODA: *They will drag us down, we have larger dreams, remaking a society / a world, we should choose the best, only the best, why serve everyone –*

MARY: *Love the prodigal, the dull, the narrow, help them –*

VIRGINIA: *Give us small comforts, a glass of gin, the liquid burning my throat, feeding my fancies, a drink / a drink a drink a drink, my liver is burning, thirsty thirsty a drink a drink a drink a drink a drink –*

MONICA: *Men balance the world, men as Darwin sees them achieving / succeeding and winning, their deep calm voices, their feet planted in the ground –*

RHODA: *Women with intelligence and ambition to succeed, achieve and win / willing to climb forbidden mountains –*

MARY: *Encourage and praise and prod and love, never give up, all worthy, all full of hidden treasure –*

ALICE: *We must get out –*

VIRGINIA: *We'll never get out –*

MARY: *The younger one is pretty and the older ones will love me.*

SCENE 6: GYNECOLOGIST

A medical examination room with an examination table, one chair and a stool. A small utility table holds medical instruments, a washing basin and towel.

Mary sits on the examining table.
Rhoda sits near her.
Everard appears.

EVERARD: Cousin Mary, you look exactly the same as when I left.

MARY: You look older. It's all that exotic travelling.

EVERARD: You took over three weeks to answer my note. I was looking forward to dining with you again, arguing till the wee hours –

MARY: My pardon. The school is a very large endeavour.

EVERARD: Dear Mary, I have no idea why you insisted on my examining you. London is full of doctors.

MARY: Sadists. My last doctor was in the habit of performing clitoridectomies as a cure for excessive nerves.

EVERARD: Not on you, I presume.

MARY: Dr. Elizabeth Garrett is overwhelmed and three other physicians have refused to treat me. All I ask is that you give me fair warning when it is time for the speculum. There's a reckless use of that instrument among your profession.

EVERARD: It isn't my profession. I haven't practiced for years. I was always more of a dilettante scientist, and now I've given up even that. Now sit still while I listen to your heart ... pray relax yourself.

MARY: Impossible.

EVERARD: (*listening to his stethoscope*) Strong and even.

MARY: I tell women to be examined once yearly and I must be an example.

EVERARD: After returning from my travels, I hoped to visit you for a good meal, not to examine your nether regions.

MARY: Reproductive system. And you will visit, Everard. Soon.

EVERARD: Miss Nunn, do you also wish to be examined?

MARY: She has already had her appointment.

RHODA: I've already had my appointment.

EVERARD: Ah.

Everard returns the stethoscope to the table.

MARY: Do you still believe that women in menopause automatically become nymphomaniacs?

EVERARD: I no longer believe in automatic ovario-uterine excitement.

MARY: Good.

EVERARD: Or in the wandering-uterus theory.

Everard covers Mary's lower half with a sheet.

MARY: Even better.

EVERARD: But there are indications that child-bearing capacities are compromised by too much thinking. Now, lie down.

Mary lies down on the examining table. She faces away from the audience.

As vital energy is drawn away to support the intellect, the ovaries wither.

MARY: Yes, I am nature, of the body, while you are culture, of the intellect. This creates, for women, a diabolical collapsing of physical function and social creation.

Everard begins palpating Mary's lower abdomen.

EVERARD: To challenge these distinctions is to go against our inherent sex natures.

MARY: I've been unsexing myself for years – be careful down there.

EVERARD: (*feeling her, completely professional*) Mmhuhh, ahhh … yes, against our inherent natures, which involve all qualities of behaviour. The manner in which we smell a rose. Now breasts.

Everard checks Mary's breasts, feeling them in a circular motion.

And as women's nerve centres are in a greater state of instability, they are more easily deranged.

RHODA: I've heard that everything is allied – our brains, nerves, muscles, organs.

EVERARD: She speaks.

RHODA: I draw my brain away from my womb and I am free to reason.

EVERARD: And how do you accomplish that?

RHODA: By concentrating my thoughts.

EVERARD: Ah.

MARY: These breasts have been palpated enough.

Everard moves to a utility table to retrieve his speculum.

EVERARD: But you are built to bear children.

RHODA: And you are built to hunt bison.

EVERARD: Fair warning, Mary. Now, the speculum.

Everard sits at the end of the table on a small stool, facing the audience.

Move down. Farther …

Mary moves her bottom down towards Everard. Her knees are apart, the sheet covers her.

Farther …

MARY: Oh God.

Everard ducks underneath the sheet, covering his head. He peeks out at times to speak.

EVERARD: Good. You see, the cervix is comparable to the tonsils, the womb has a neck and a throat.

Everard inserts the speculum.

RHODA: Then you might as well look down her mouth.

MARY: Couldn't the instrument be warmed?

EVERARD: Then visit a real physician.

MARY: Real physicians place it in ice.

EVERARD: Huhmmh ... ahha (*pulling out the speculum*) Gently, gently ... Mary, you are a paragon of health.

MARY: I need a glass of wine.

EVERARD: I could do with a whole bottle. This is a borrowed office, but there is always some port for the fainters. I'll wash up and then we'll celebrate our reunion. Wine calms the nerves even better than a hysterectomy. Ladies, a joke – *Why has she done this, why act out doctor and patient, I feel as if I had been examined, as if she wanted to test me before her protege* – Cousin Mary, you've chosen an odd way to introduce me to your protege.

Everard wheels the small table away as he exits.

RHODA: *Utterly odd.*

MARY: (*calling after Everard*) This is not an introduction, it is a business appointment – *If she was going to meet my comely cousin, better in a borrowed office, an instrument of torture in his hand –*

RHODA: He's not a monster.

MARY: I never said he was.

RHODA: You did.

MARY: You see a handsome man, intelligent, well-spoken, one who's suffered in the mysterious fashion that travelling brings on. But he has been a rogue and may remain one.

RHODA: Rogues are immoral.

MARY: Men are immoral. Perhaps I feel some guilt. Everard's father objected to his roguish behaviour and changed his will. Everard received enough to live fairly well, but most of the inheritance came to me.

RHODA: That's how you got the school. I didn't know. Do you feel you owe him something?

MARY: I owe him nothing.

Everard enters with wine and glasses in hand. He pours for the ladies.

EVERARD: Miss Nunn, you know that I am in sympathy with your cause.

MARY: Bollocks.

EVERARD: Mary went to jail so often that, as a youth, I was unable to shock our family.

MARY: You managed to shock.

EVERARD: And paid for it.

MARY: You did.

EVERARD: To the New Woman.

They drink.

You see, you ladies are actually working for the betterment of men. The majority of women are poor creatures, dependent, wracked with nerves. They want to trap men into marriage, then nag them to the grave. What's an intelligent man to do? Where can he find a mate? In the New Woman, who can converse intelligently and who doesn't rely on love to provide all inner resolve. You are creating better wives for my future.

MARY: It's a buyer's market in wives right now.

EVERARD: Oh, I'll never marry. I've seen too many hounded men.

RHODA: I too will never marry.

EVERARD: You might still be asked.

RHODA: I am not waiting to be asked.

MARY: Rhoda is truly a New Woman.

EVERARD: She hates men.

RHODA: She sees men for what they are.

EVERARD: Selfish, dominating –

RHODA: Beings that need to be woken up.

EVERARD: Then wake us up.

RHODA: I am in the business of waking up the women, you should wake up the men.

EVERARD: But I need help.

RHODA: I need none.

MARY: I don't approve of the way you approve of us. Everard, we must go. You may be a man of leisure but we are working women.

EVERARD: *My doodle is stirred again, that pretty girl in the park was very sweet, but women like this, old and young, hawkish and proud, the thought of lifting their skirts and seeking out the moist folds beneath, of bringing brilliant heady women to their knees moaning, grasping at me –*

RHODA: *A comely man of thirty-five, the sight of him, the fact he is large, that I would feel small, that I could sink into him tiny and kept, protected and loved, I am spinning, spinning towards him –*

MARY: *Refuse him entry, tell him he's not allowed, no comely young men allowed here –*

EVERARD: Now that I've proven myself by playing the doctor, may I visit if I am very good? I do admire you. I didn't need heroes when I was growing up, I had glorious Mary.

MARY: You are welcome to visit, Everard. *Why, why do I say it?*

EVERARD: Thank you, cousin. I'll expect an invitation to dinner. Miss Nunn. Until we meet again.

SCENE 7: THE INSTRUCTION

Mary Barfoot's sitting room.
The Remingtons are lined up,
shining metallic in the light.
Rhoda, Virginia and Alice stand in front of them.

ALICE: They seem rather ferocious.

VIRGINIA: Violent, yet lonely.

RHODA: They're not lonely. They feel nothing. They are machines.

ALICE: Lonely.

VIRGINIA: Definitely.

ALICE: Evil?

VIRGINIA: Perhaps.

RHODA: Then the first step will be to become familiar with them. We will merely look at the Remingtons.

Virginia turns away, we see her take a mickey from her pocket and have a slug of brandy.

ALICE: Look, as in regard? Regard an instrument of torture, a cold clattering mechanism? It will pinch my fingers, make me feel stupid. We are beset with constant new devices and inventions –

VIRGINIA: So exciting. I am so invigorated by this ... by ... the keys which seem to be moving by themselves, weaving like stiff fingers pointing out of a shallow grave.

RHODA: I'm teaching you separately so that you can catch up with the other girls.

ALICE: Girls? Are they all girls?

RHODA: Women, the other women.

ALICE: But we are older than the others.

RHODA: Monica isn't older, and after she settles into her room, she'll join us.

ALICE: It is the new, you see, Miss Nunn –

RHODA: Rhoda, please.

ALICE: We are always behind, unsuited and unfit, those who are able to keep up and those who cannot. I want to shout, 'Stop, this quickness will kill us all!' But no one listens, and I don't shout or speak. Ohh, ohhh – *I'm burning, bones melting, molten lava, drenched in sweat* –

RHODA: What is it? You're perspiring / so profusely.

VIRGINIA: Is it the –

ALICE: Twice this morning already, and all last night.

RHODA: A fever?

ALICE: My younger self is being burned out of me … it's passing.

RHODA: But what is it? Malaria? The flux? Should we call a doctor?

ALICE: Women change, it will happen to you.

VIRGINIA: We bleed, and then we burn.

ALICE: And burn and burn.

RHODA: Oh. I see. We should start working.

ALICE: *It'll happen to her one day, one day she'll start to burn, her womb will burn, her heart and limbs, her nerves shrivelling in the flame –*

VIRGINIA: I wish to train my mind and heart to be independent and strong, like you, Rhoda. I can feel a change already. Do you see it in my countenance?

ALICE: We have always worked hard, but it is the fear, you see. Instinctive female fear.

VIRGINIA: Inbred tremulousness, inbred nervous agonies.

RHODA: Enough gazing. Now you will touch the Remingtons.

They touch them.

VIRGINIA: Oh God.

RHODA: What?

VIRGINIA: Metal.

ALICE: *Conducting heat and cold / malleable and ductile –*

VIRGINIA: *Coursing through me, chemical combinations –*

RHODA: Now the basic keys. Have you ever had piano lessons?

ALICE: A few, but Father felt it was too much for Virginia.

RHODA: Think of the type machine as a literary piano. Begin by pressing the keys at random, to get the feel of them.

They do.

VIRGINIA: It makes no impression.

RHODA: Press harder. (*showing her*)

VIRGINIA: My fingers pain me. You see, still nothing.

RHODA: Harder. Alice, keep your wrists even.

VIRGINIA: Alice's wrists aren't even.

ALICE: My fingers bend in an odd way, you see, at the ends? It makes pressing firmly very difficult. Our father used to say I was born for a life of ease.

RHODA: Like this –

ALICE: Oh yes, that's a little better.

RHODA: You will memorize this chart, which refers to the position of the keys.

VIRGINIA: Memorize the chart.

RHODA: Then we'll add shorthand, dictation and / correspondence –

VIRGINIA: Good, of course, shorthand and dictation and more, I hope there is more. Much more.

ALICE: And we'll learn all this in just six months?

RHODA: Perhaps a little longer. We'll start with the basic position of the hands. Hold your hands just above the keys ... without pressing the keys, merely hold them –

Alice and Virginia continue to play with the keys.

RHODA: If you could refrain from pressing the keys for a moment.

Alice and Virginia continue to play with the keys.

Stop pressing the ...! Thank you. Settle yourselves. Now look at the first diagram. Extend your fingers –

VIRGINIA: I've slipped again.

RHODA: Then try again. Press each finger in succession from left to right –

ALICE: *We're very bad, you should punish us –*

VIRGINIA: *Father used to spank us when we were naughty –*

ALICE: *We were always the better for it –*

VIRGINIA: *It / hurt him more than it hurt us –*

ALICE: *He made us work harder –*

VIRGINIA: *We were always slow –*

RHODA: *You want me to dominate the room, dominate the teaching, dominate you poor excuses for women, who remind me of every lack-lustre female relative –*

VIRGINIA: I cannot learn, I do not understand (*begins to cry*). It is hopeless, hopeless. How can I imagine myself working in an office, a boss of a man watching over me, telling me I do it wrong, criticizing constantly and buzzing around me, like bees with quick fingers, well-dressed ambitious young people, bred of machines, born of machines, who is that faded old maid, she can't keep up, she can't keep up!

RHODA: We'll proceed more slowly.

ALICE: Dear, you've exerted yourself too much. Miss Nunn, perhaps we could rest a while?

RHODA: I understand that both of you are in poor health but –

ALICE: Poor health? Our muscles ache, our energy is sapped, our nerves are raw strips of flesh, our self-respect rots in an old hope chest as beetles and worms eat our girlish dreams.

VIRGINIA: Why didn't Father see to it that we were fit for something!

ALICE: Father? What has Father to do with learning / to use a type machine –

VIRGINIA: We can't even teach school properly. Did he think our great beauty and brilliant conversation would buy us husbands?

ALICE: You are desecrating our father's memory!

RHODA: Fathers want their daughters to be compliant / feminine in the sense of –

ALICE: What do you know?

RHODA: I know how to typewrite.

Rhoda begins typing under ...

VIRGINIA: Where are they? Where are the men? Why now, of all the ages of the world, are women left so alone? We are slaves, ignorant and fearful, degraded, raped and pillaged –

ALICE: You don't even understand the ideas you are parroting / they're making you hysterical.

VIRGINIA: Humiliated! Forsaken! / Battered! Beaten!

ALICE: Hysterical mania!

RHODA: Type, damn you. Type! It's the way to liberty!

VIRGINIA: I cannot live. I can't earn enough to keep from starving! Why shouldn't I be / hysterical?

RHODA: Now I am hysterical!

ALICE: You have murdered our peace!

Virginia runs out of the room.

Virginia!

Alice runs after Virginia.

RHODA: *An odd woman cries out to God that she's been robbed of children, robbed of a husband's love, robbed of the joys of amorous union. God answers that she has been abandoned in order to rise up and challenge all that has ever been. Is that what I believe? What do I believe?*

Everard's apartment.
He stands gazing out a window,
naked except for a silk kimono,
speaking to someone in the next room.

EVERARD: Traditional society regarded women as sexually treacherous and insatiable. Modern society regards them as sexually pure and passionless. Now we have the science of sexology to discover the sex truth. But they have barely begun to enlighten us. There should be a Sexologist Exhibition, a circumstance for people to match with each other – large signs proclaim the categories of desire. A brightly coloured sign proclaims 'Sex Act but No Love' – a like-minded crowd gathers. Sexologists scurry after them to make notations.

Monica enters in bloomers and chemise – she snuggles into Everard.

Another large coloured sign, 'Love but no Sex Act.' How many would gather, I wonder?

MONICA: One would say 'Spanking and Worse.'

EVERARD: 'Touching and Holding Only.'

MONICA: One would say 'Frig Me into the Ground.'

EVERARD: Once a shrinking virgin, now a wild woman.

MONICA: Oh God, what would my sisters say if they heard me? If they saw me?

EVERARD: *I couldn't help myself, such a luscious creature, about to be initiated by someone, and after a few encounters, a true participant –*

MONICA: *There is still time to save yourself, leap out the window, run through the streets in your bloomers, confess to a priest – dear Father, I am at the mercy of my flesh, it speaks to me at night, I cannot tame it, even though hell waits for me –* Why aren't you married?

EVERARD: I love freedom.

MONICA: So do I, but at the shop I saw girls who were free but common. I don't wish to be common even if I am free.

EVERARD: Don't bother your uncommon little brain. Just rest, while this great strong man holds you in his arms. Next Sunday then?

MONICA: Next Sunday I will drain your coffers dry.

SCENE 9: THE FIGHT

Mary Barfoot's sitting room.
Rhoda paces,
Mary takes her hand, begins to
massage her shoulders.

MARY: You're restless again.

RHODA: It's the three sisters.

MARY: You've been fighting with them. You've been rude.

RHODA: Yes, Mary. Forgive me, Mary.

MARY: You must apologize.

RHODA: I will not.

MARY: They will find work, especially Monica. These women are no worse than many we've taught.

RHODA: Why send out hopeless cases who will do the school's reputation terrible harm?

MARY: Hopeless? You taught the girl who couldn't speak above a whisper, you taught Sarah – remember Sarah with syphilis? When did you become so hard?

RHODA: *How to explain what happened when I met him, how my mind swirled, how my body thrummed, how the three sisters felt part of it all, the icy breath of change* – The school is a political and social experiment with great consequences for the movement. We must be consistent.

MARY: In a pig's arse. When has anything alive, breathing and farting ever been consistent? We must open our arms to contradiction. Find the human path.

RHODA: If you love me, get rid of them.

MARY: Throw them out to starve? You are a changeling – the Rhoda I love will return. Beware of losing your compassion.

RHODA: I feel no compassion.

MARY: In that case I will take the decision independently and allow the sisters to stay.

RHODA: Then I have no say as to what happens? Perhaps I should no longer be employed here.

MARY: You are not 'employed.'

RHODA: No, our friendship keeps it from being that, but if we were no longer friends –

MARY: No longer friends?

RHODA: I could no longer live here.

MARY: If you do not wish to be friends any longer –

RHODA: Then would I still have employment?

MARY: Of course / but –

RHODA: But it wouldn't be the same if we weren't friends. You and I are not partners –

MARY: If we use business language, yes, we are like partners –

RHODA: Not officially, not legally –

MARY: You are in my will.

RHODA: And so you have power over me, to go above my wishes for the school –

MARY: Yes, I have power, it is my school.

RHODA: Then what am I?

MARY: You are my ... you are my –

RHODA: I see, I see it all clearly. If I have a different opinion than yours, I am hard and inhuman.

MARY: Yes, inhuman – I look for a shred of womanly grace –

RHODA: But you are weak. Giving in to 'womanly' sentiment and weeping emotions. Weak, weak, weak.

MARY: How dare you / call me weak?

RHODA: Perhaps you are correct in your self-criticism, perhaps you are a coward.

MARY: I have withstood torture / I have –

RHODA: Deserting the true cause, afraid / of real struggle. A coward.

MARY: I could tear your hair out / for that.

RHODA: Tear away. Or I'll pack my bags first.

Monica enters and stands watching, unseen.

MARY: Pack 'em quickly or I'll show you what I learned in prison!

RHODA: Go ahead / I said do your worst.

MARY: I must get out before I do something horrific.

Mary storms out.
Monica comes fully into the room.

MONICA: I am ready for my lesson. But perhaps you are occupied with something horrific.

RHODA: Why did you come here?

MONICA: To sit on the lap of my employer, to blackmail him to his wife, to gain entry into a forbidden world and suck it for all I can. Isn't that what you think?

RHODA: Please be seated at the type machine.

MONICA: You're not really all that plain, you know.

RHODA: *Plain from Mary, plain from this flirty cow –*

MONICA: And you laugh more than I thought, I caught you laughing with Mary.

RHODA: *Laughing with Mary –*

MONICA: *She'll soon see that I'm not wicked, or, if I am wicked, she will punish me, punish the part of me that will meet him to fuse breaths, tongues, skins, to share that piercing joy, that suddenly cares nothing of what anyone thinks –* My sisters ruined me. They made me half a / lady and –

RHODA: So you keep saying. I only see the shopgirl – *So appallingly ripe, while I am rotting on the vine.*

MONICA: Bluestockings are supposed to be virtuous and kind – *at night I touch and rub myself even if it will make me blind, I am being driven to madness –*

RHODA: *She's exuding an animal scent, feral and fecund and fertile –* Sit down at the type machine.

MONICA: You are against marriage, but what do you think of a girl marrying to help not only her own situation but that of others?

RHODA: Press the keys in order left to right. The third finger on the left hand is the most difficult to strengthen.

MONICA: The marriage finger.

RHODA: Then marry. Give over to servitude, ravishment and theft. Become a sex slave.

MONICA: What if I wish to be a sex slave? Women seek it, they must want it –

RHODA: In the future, it will be possible to exist with a man as an equal.

MONICA: When in the future?

RHODA: In thirty years. By 1915.

MONICA: Thirty years … I'll be fifty!

RHODA: Pray excuse me, the lesson is finished. We will make it up at another time.

MONICA: You're protected by Miss Barfoot – she is the husband and you are the wife.

RHODA: I told her she shouldn't let you in.

MONICA: She was bored. She needed new blood.

As Rhoda exits.

Don't go. You wouldn't use a man to escape a life of drudgery? You would, I know you would!

Virginia staggers in, very drunk.

MONICA: Virgie.

VIRGINIA: I must have fallen … I haven't been well, just risen from a nap, the schooling here is very rigorous. I must practice, the Remington seems / to be broken …

MONICA: Virgie, are you …?

VIRGINIA: You notice a smell perhaps? I had to ask Miss Barfoot for a little medicine, I felt rather faint –

MONICA: It's brandy.

Virginia crawls underneath the Remington looking for a hidden mickey.

VIRGINIA: Yes, I told you. The machine is broken, Rhoda fixes them with a great wrench – *Lord, I've got a head on me like a forty-shilling pisspot* –

MONICA: *None of us will say it, that my sister reeks of drink, that my sister's mind is sodden* –

VIRGINIA: *Poor little slut, dear little angel* –

Virginia finds her bottle.

MONICA: Virgie, you've had a terrible time, really.

VIRGINIA: Not at all. There is sometimes a feeling of emptiness, a desire for … a kind of laughter.

MONICA: I used to make you laugh.

VIRGINIA: You were a laughing child – *A little girl jumps up and down, she pokes at us, lifting her skirts, laughing and laughing* –

MONICA: *My sister's hands, lifting me carefully, pressing their palms against my mouth, quiet, dear, shshhhhhh, smelling of lye and lavender* –

VIRGINIA: (*begins crying*) Alice dislikes me now. All our lives we've been like two peas in a pod and now we're barely speaking. She resists the new theories while I have become very revolutionary … Sometimes I think I should go to Berlin and learn to smoke and wear trousers.

MONICA: Wherever did you get that idea?

VIRGINIA: In a house of New Women there are always lots of pamphlets.

MONICA: I will repay you for all your sacrifices – *for the papery caresses, the feeling that I'll owe you forever as you sink lower and lower –*

VIRGINIA: I'll sleep a bit. Perhaps right here. *Dear little tart, dear little grubbian –*

Virginia lies down on the floor, her head in Monica's lap. Monica strokes her hair.

… Cash out my share of the principal and take … the night train … to Berlin …

SCENE 10: WEEPING WOMAN AND HANDKERCHIEF

A park bench.
A dull day.
Rhoda sits miserably, she's been crying.
Everard enters.

EVERARD: Miss Nunn. I've just called at the house. Mary was unable to see me. Is she ill?

RHODA: A headache perhaps.

EVERARD: Your eyes look quite red.

RHODA: It's the fog.

EVERARD: It makes your eyes weep.

RHODA: No one is weeping!

EVERARD: Of course not – *For God's sake be calm, I'm not here to steal your virtue.*

RHODA: Mr. Barfoot, I wish to be alone.

EVERARD: Of course.

Everard sits down beside Rhoda.

It seemed Mary was upset.

RHODA: I am upset.

EVERARD: Then you admit it.

RHODA: Mary is the more upset.

EVERARD: You and my cousin are much more than mistress and employee, you are ...

RHODA: What? What are we?

EVERARD: Friends. Good women friends.

RHODA: *What is his idea of women friends, girlish talks with tea and biscuits? Can he imagine breast against breast in the night?*

EVERARD: *She seems less plain than before, a glow of intelligent unhappiness, so different from unintelligent unhappiness* – Miss Nunn, I am a bit of an occultist, I detect frequencies about you. There has been a disturbance between you and Mary.

RHODA: I'm afraid we may have to part.

EVERARD: You and I?

RHODA: Mary and I.

EVERARD: Surely not.

RHODA: I've grown hard, she thinks me hard ... (*begins sobbing*)

EVERARD: (*offering handkerchief*) Allow me.

RHODA: *The horrible banality, weeping woman and handkerchief, stop, I cannot stop, I said malicious things and now she doesn't love me –* She doesn't love me.

EVERARD: Of course she loves you. You and Mary aren't ordinary women who tear each other's hair and have snits and gossip evil about each other – *I know how to comfort her, the warmth is pouring out of me, I am aroused by a bluestocking with a red nose –*

RHODA: Everything we've built is at risk if unsuitable or immoral girls, women, are sent out.

EVERARD: I agree, throw out the chaff, teach the wheat dictation.

RHODA: Why do you assume I am in the right? *His hands are long and white.*

EVERARD: Because I admire you.

RHODA: There's no logic in that –

EVERARD: *The swell of her breasts –*

RHODA: *The bulge in his trousers –*

EVERARD: I wish to see your cause succeed.

RHODA: Mary understands our cause better than any woman alive – *Mary, who I betray in my thoughts –*

EVERARD: I only meant … that the cause shouldn't be served only by unmarried women – *That doesn't follow, why did I say it?*

RHODA: Of course not – *That doesn't follow, why did he say it?*

EVERARD: I understand that you want the fair sex to control their own purses, even when they're married. I need – *An heiress with a swollen, bulging purse –*

RHODA: What do you need?

EVERARD: Stimulation.

RHODA: I have a stimulating life.

EVERARD: And yet you are unfulfilled. Scientifically unfulfilled.

RHODA: Scientifically?

EVERARD: Physically.

RHODA: What if I said that I was physically fulfilled? *Why suddenly does it seem untrue? Far down in me a swelling, an arching –*

EVERARD: You are an odd woman, so I assume that … I presume that – *that she is hymen intacta at the very least, yet she has the smell, the look of, no, not quite, not quite a virgin –* Forgive me, I am a mere mortal gazing at a warrior maid. Artemis of the type machines.

RHODA: Women have travelled a great way, our lives are nobler and richer than they were, but they are also fiendishly difficult. We are cruelly bruised as we reach for the light.

EVERARD: How beautifully you speak your ideas / how beautifully –

RHODA: And now, if you please, I will take my leave. Your hand-kerchief will be returned –

Everard takes Rhoda's hand.

I will not sleep with it under my pillow, hold it to my heart, rub it between my, between my legs –

EVERARD: Miss Nunn, if I have offended you in any way –

RHODA: Pray release my hand –

EVERARD: A strong hand. You make no attempt to attract male attention and that in itself is attractive.

RHODA: I don't expect or desire male admiration. *True, completely true, almost true, true till this moment …*

EVERARD: *She will desire me, I'll make her twitch and buck –*

Everard releases Rhoda's hand.

RHODA: Mr. Barfoot.

EVERARD: Always a pleasure, Miss Nunn.

SCENE 11: REHEARSING AND FAINTING

Mary Barfoot's sitting room.
Mary reads from a typewritten speech.
Alice, Monica, Virginia sit expectantly.
Rhoda stands in the shadows.

MARY: Last night I slept not at all. I awoke from a fantasy. I realized we have been utterly wrong in everything we have fought for. We must abandon all reforms for women before we do irreparable harm. We are creating abominations. The financial dependence of women stems from our reproductive capacities. It is of the natural order. We are weaker! Our minds buckle, our nerves fray, our friendships wither when put to the test. When we enter men's realm of ambition we become hard and uncaring. While a man may be his natural self as he competes for power, we lose our very souls. Instead of altering the fabric of business as we enter it, we imitate its worst transgressions, trampling our poorer sisters for a few extra pence. Ay, we unsex ourselves and disrupt the balance of the world in the name of many freedoms which do not lead to liberation but are dangerous indulgences with consequences beyond knowing. The way ahead is full of shame, of tears and terror, of wild love and losses so deep they have no name. We will watch society crack with our freedom. Go back to your homes, you stupid women. It is over.

Pause. Uncomprehending applause from Virginia and Alice. Monica claps with less enthusiasm. Rhoda still watches in the shadows.

VIRGINIA: I am speechless, I am stirred. I want to, I don't know what I want to do. Alice?

ALICE: I feel as if I have walked upside down or swallowed a large building. Monica, what do you think?

MONICA: Is that the speech you're going to give at the rally?

MARY: Why ever not? *So tired of mouthing the same old arguments, don't give a rat's arse anymore, blah blah blah –*

MONICA: How could you mean it? You challenge us with negation.

MARY: Do I?

MONICA: Was it done for effect?

MARY: Let women lie down and be tramped on for all I care – *Still mouthing, still, blah blah –*

MONICA: But you cannot believe that women should abandon / all that has been –

VIRGINIA: Yes, we are challenged to counter your assumptions which are, which are –

ALICE: I am experiencing a shortness of breath –

MONICA: I see what has happened. Your cause has ignored inconvenient truths. Now you see the effect of your revolution and you pale.

MARY: In my darkest hours I do pale –

MONICA: Deny marriage and stir up women –

MARY: We do not deny the importance of family –

MONICA: The balance of the world is already upset and these 'dangerous indulgences' are erotical freedoms which naturally result from what you have set in motion –

MARY: You've been reading the books I suggested.

MONICA: One or two.

MARY: We have ignored some aspects of – provocative girl –

MONICA: Erotical freedoms are historically inseparable from the discourse of liberation.

MARY: True, often true. Devious minx. But the real danger is our own weakness – we must speak more –

Rhoda joins the group.

RHODA: My congratulations, Mary. The speech is brilliant, shocking, horrifying even.

MARY: I don't even know what I said. *I know exactly what I said, anger fuels the brain –*

RHODA: *I could never leave you –*

MARY: *Liar –*

MONICA: Pardon me, Mary and I were conversing.

RHODA: And now Mary and I are conversing.

MONICA: *Is something moist going on? Is it possible they're smashed on each other?*

ALICE: I believe they're setting up the buffet. Let us freshen up. No one will miss us.

VIRGINIA: *You will miss me, dear mouldy old Alice, I am taking destiny in my hand and booking the night train to Berlin –*

Alice and Virginia exit.

MONICA: I've met a man.

RHODA: Of course you have.

MONICA: If I were a New Woman, would I have to marry him in order to explore my bodily desires?

MARY: There is no unified doctrine –

RHODA: You must think. That is what we're trying to teach women to do –

MARY: If you are to act upon your appetites, at least use a cundum.

MONICA: A what?

RHODA: A cundum. Available at the druggists.

MARY: A French letter, a Spanish bull cup.

RHODA: A Russian pot holder.

MARY: They're made of sheep intestines and the man pulls it over his member, with some difficulty / and there it sits, protecting –

MONICA: No man would do any such thing –

Alice runs in, a train schedule in her hand.
Virginia follows.

VIRGINIA: Alice!

ALICE: Miss Barfoot, what did you know of this? Virginia says she is going to Berlin of all places on God's earth.

MARY: Berlin, why Berlin?

MONICA: Are you really going?

ALICE: You knew? Did everyone know?

VIRGINIA: No one knew.

MONICA: She said something when she was in the drink. Oh, Virgie, I didn't mean to –

MARY: Yes, the drink. Alice, did you hear what Monica said?

ALICE: She has broken into the principal! Stolen money from the principal!

VIRGINIA: Stolen my own third!

RHODA: Alice, the medicine your sister has been taking is brandy and gin.

VIRGINIA: How can you suggest such unladylike behaviour? I have been ill, very ill –

MARY: Do you deny it?

ALICE: Is this true? Virginia?

VIRGINIA: I'm cronked most of the time, I slather for it. I sneak to the bar at the train station and drink with prostitutes and sailors, I drink in our room, on the street, I lie beneath the Remingtons and lap it up like a mangy dog. It makes me feel that my life is grand / and exuberant, that my life isn't wasted –

ALICE: She starved herself to buy liquor and now she is running away.

VIRGINIA: I have tried to stop, you don't know how I have tried, but I am in its grip.

ALICE: You will get on a train by yourself? Go off to a foreign place by yourself?

VIRGINIA: I must do something radical!

MARY: Berlin can be a dangerous place –

ALICE: You are incapable of any such action.

VIRGINIA: Yes, the schedules and timetables will be wearying and difficult / perhaps ...

ALICE: You'd leave me alone? – *I will tear your hair out first, I will go to lawyers and leave you destitute, I will bite you in the stomach, I will watch your spleen and liver spill to the ground and devour them, I will devour you, burp you out* – I know you, sister, I know the melancholia that drives you to deaden your senses. Do you think you won't meet the same feelings even if you travel to the ends of the earth?

MARY: Perhaps you should stop the drink first, then go on a small holiday / perhaps the seaside –

VIRGINIA: But I must be large, a small holiday / would be meaningless–

RHODA: Virginia, if you wish to alter your habits –

VIRGINIA: I am being hounded by feminist persons! Help! / Someone, help!

ALICE: Years together, helping you find employment, supporting you mentally while you were drinking like a navvy, I have had opportunities –

VIRGINIA: With men? Ha! Not a single ... cock has ever come near you.

ALICE: With you around, what ... cock would dare?

VIRGINIA: I feel faint –

ALICE: Faint, then.

VIRGINIA: I am going to faint.

ALICE: Do you think I cannot faint? I will faint first. Observe. I pant with shame and betrayal, and then ... ahhhh ...

Alice faints.

VIRGINIA: Shame and betrayal? I faint from the weighty chains of sisterly love! Ahhhhhhh!

Virginia faints.

MONICA: Chains? Pretty Monica, what would she know of chains? I'll faint – wait. Why faint at all if there's no man to catch you? *Am I a nymphomaniac?*

RHODA: We faint because our corsets are too tight, we faint because we're encouraged to take no exercise –

MARY: I'd love to faint.

RHODA: No, not you.

MARY: To sink, to flutter, to be caught. Then, if the faint is real, to vomit in someone's hat.

RHODA: Women feign weakness to barter for security which creates loneliness – oh, go ahead.

MARY: It isn't easy to fall to the ground, I'll have to do it in stages ... ahh ... ahh .... ahhhhh ...

Mary faints.

So voluptuous to be feeble –

MONICA: I will faint better than any of you. I pale delightfully, I waver, but recover, then slip gracefully ... ahhhh.

Monica faints.

ALICE: (*from the floor*) I feel ridiculous.

VIRGINIA: I feel sublime.

MONICA: Rhoda, you must faint too.

RHODA: But what am I fainting from?

MARY: The sheer weight of the Woman Question.

RHODA: Oh yes, it is a weight, a boulder of mammoth proportions ... I wobble –

MONICA: Not so stiff.

RHODA: I surrender, I allow a desperate yet pleasantly overwhelming / giddiness to ... yes ... almost ... almost ... ah ... ah.

VIRGINIA: Yes! / Keep it up!

MARY: Yes! More / surrendering!

MONICA: You can do it!

RHODA: Ah ah ahhhhhh –

Rhoda faints.
All the women lie fetchingly on the floor.
Enter Everard.

EVERARD: No one answered the door. Rhoda? Monica? What is happening here?

MARY: We have all fainted.

He regards the women.

EVERARD: Men aren't afraid of women, really, only of women in groups.

INTERMISSION

ACT 2

SCENE 12: IMPRESSIONISTS

The first Impressionist exhibition in London.
The characters are shocked,
yet exhilarated by the paintings.
They move in pools of light,
hanging on to their programs for dear life.

Everard alone but near Monica.
Mary, Alice and Rhoda form a group.

EVERARD: *Impressionism! Impressions of objects, impressions of figures, impressions of impressions – vulgar mockery or painterly inspiration? –*

ALICE: *Scrawls and splatters, indecipherable chaos, my eyes lose focus, the floor tilts, there is no ground under my feet, unfinished, completely unfinished –*

MONICA: *Rough and bold, vibrant and free, a leap into the unknown / freedom from form, freedom from construction –*

MARY: *Subversion, emancipation from rigid structures / the abandoning of all tradition –*

RHODA: *Blotches of water, a twist of parasol, no clear lines / no depth or projection, the flaming of light and dust, a level of enchantment –*

ALICE: *Smear a panel with grey, plonk some black and yellow lines, dot it with red and blue blobs / violent, loud, clumsy, naked brush strokes, tortured nature, great gaps of nothingness, subverting all sense of delicacy, of beauty –*

EVERARD: *Imperfect, deliberately imperfect, shadowy elusiveness / transience, nothing fixed, nothing certain –*

RHODA: *All is movement, combustion and flux / flickering and insubstantial –*

MONICA: *Seething, wavering, waving, ravishing shimmerings of light and shade, bursting forth with colour –*

MARY: *The world is now divided into two, those who can stand these wild impressions and those who cannot bear to see the shapes within.*

Everard notices Monica.

EVERARD: Miss Monica, I never thought to see you here.

MONICA: The exhibition of the century and you think me too simple to know it?

EVERARD: No, not at all, I / merely –

MONICA: An astounding eruption of new vision and yet these artists are called primitive.

EVERARD: You've changed since I last saw you, and not merely in your dress. Are you here alone?

MONICA: I came with a friend. A gentleman. There, by the ballerina with the heavy legs.

EVERARD: And there is mysterious Rhoda Nunn.

MONICA: Mysterious as a plank.

EVERARD: He looks very posh. Who is he?

MONICA: Keep your eyes on the paintings or my friend will interrupt us.

RHODA: (*to Mary*) There's Monica. With Everard. *Monica with Everard, Monica with Everard, he leans towards her as if ready to pluck her breasts and bite –*

MARY: Monica seems to have lost interest in the school.

RHODA: She rarely attends class, comes and goes as she pleases, and gives out that she's engaged, although to whom is unclear.

ALICE: In just four months she has had at least two fiancés. I won't join her yet, she's speaking with Everard. He is a good influence on her, so steady, so remote. Her present fiancé seems more impressionable –

MARY: Who is this fiancé?

ALICE: Monica is much admired –

RHODA: But where does she go?

ALICE: An engaged woman has many duties and responsibilities – *The pain is blinding, why can no one see it, my heart shrieks with loneliness, it is eating my soul like a scabrous disease –*

EVERARD: (*to Monica*) I have every respect for what you are, or have become, but since spending time with Rhoda and Mary, I've become aware that some aspects of male behaviour are not … are quite … I am ashamed of my behaviour toward you.

MONICA: Ashamed? *Ashamed of our lusty afternoons, of the curve of my flank, the soft hair of my feather, you'll not see me weep –* Those women have unsexed you, you're soft as a girl, you weren't like that when we sneaked into your rooms, when you licked me like a cat –

EVERARD: The instinct of the female is resistance, then if she is won, surrender. This keeps a balance in nature –

MONICA: You poor booby. As you speak, the world explores free lovism.

EVERARD: Free lovism? Are you practicing free lovism? I've heard there is a colony of them outside London –

MONICA: Physical liberty is the personal expression of revolutionary change – *I know the glory of my quim* –

Monica moves away from Everard.
Alice and Mary together.

ALICE: In spite of your philosophies, Mary, you must resent these artists rending the world asunder.

MARY: Oh yes, I resent it, even as I adore them. *Dining with Rhoda and Everard night after night, she getting sharper and sharper and he beginning to burn like the sun.*

Mary moves to Rhoda.

RHODA: Nut-brown women on yellow horses in forests of blue trees –

Everard and Monica.

EVERARD: (*to Monica*) I suddenly realize how alone I am, I weep easily, look, here's a tear – I can no longer speak to my male friends, the married ones are miserable, the unmarried speak about women in a fashion that now seems despicable. My head aches, I have pains in my stomach, in my liver –

MONICA: *Piss on his liver, he is like me, hot arsed, lewd and lubricious – but a coward.*

EVERARD: But are you practicing free lovism?

Monica moves to the next painting.
Mary and Rhoda.

MARY: Why do you ignore Everard?

RHODA: I'm not ignoring him. From a distance the patterns are clear but go closer and all that is recognizable disappears.

MARY: These artists have been vilified yet their ardour has not been dampened.

Monica and Everard.

MONICA: I believe our true natures to be multi-amorous – I have a few good friends, like that very learned gentleman, who support this view. I've been true to each, each I've loved, yet still I hope for –

EVERARD: For …?

MONICA: *For an end to my desires, for a housewife's cares, tiny hands clasping, a husband waiting –*

EVERARD: It is so close here, the intense colouration / the vibrating brush strokes –

Rhoda alone.

RHODA: Not a landscape but the sensation produced by a landscape –

Monica and Everard.

MONICA: You keep gazing at Rhoda – you may join her if you wish.

EVERARD: I don't know what I wish. Rhoda has ideals.

MONICA: She'd trade them all for a good match. There, my friend is getting truly impatient (*Everard again looks at Rhoda*) … and your confusion is ebbing away –

Alice crosses to Monica.

ALICE: Monica dear, I am shaken to the core, yes here is sunlight, here is water, but it wavers so. Virginia would adore this anarchy, but she has disappeared into meagre postcards marked 'Berlin.'

MONICA: She has not disappeared. And neither have I.

ALICE: Is that your fiancé? He's quite changed from when I last met him, but then my eyes aren't what they used to be. Since Virginia has gone only extremes penetrate them now.

MONICA: *I am progressive, but no whore – now I see that I am alone, completely alone.* We must go or we shall be late for an engagement. Good day, dear Alice. Mary. Rhoda. Everard.

Monica exits.

EVERARD: An unsettling exhibit.

RHODA: I find it invigorating.

MARY: *I always suspected she was a dilettante – is she an odd woman or will she be paired like any gaggle of gloves in a drawer – he is almost her match, almost –* Alice, I am determined that you recognize the rapture of this Renoir.

As Alice exits …

ALICE: Rapturous …

Mary and Alice exit.

EVERARD: You've been avoiding me. I've been visiting for over six months, but lately I dine only with Mary, you are always out with elusive friends –

RHODA: *Keep your distance or I'll scream like a stuck pig.*

EVERARD: You have spoken once or twice as if you were not quite happy with your life.

RHODA: Of course I'm not happy. What woman above the level of a petted pussy cat is happy?

EVERARD: *I would like to pet your pussy cat.*

RHODA: *Rub me, scratch me, dig your fingers into my pubis.*

EVERARD: If I'd married when I was young, I would have chosen, as the average man does, some simpleton.

RHODA: Any woman who reads the marriage contract and still gets married, deserves what she gets – *Why do I find his condescension so arousing?*

EVERARD: *She is unaware of the delights of physical union, except I suspect something vaguely Greek is going on with Mary* – I will never marry in the legal sense, my companion must be as independent of these forms as I am – A free union, however, is possible –

RHODA: *A quivering, a quickening in my loins* – In a free union, the man and woman live as one, but there is no contract, legal or religious?

EVERARD: Freedom for both. Equality for both.

RHODA: *So the women ends up with a passel of brats and no securities, while the man is free?*

EVERARD: I believe you to be my equal – do you realize the enormity of that admission?

RHODA: We fight for more than equality, we fight to endow our differences with dignity and prestige.

EVERARD: *I've got a boner so hard it's going to burst through my trousers –*

RHODA: *He's got a boner so hard it's going to burst through his trousers –* I'll see the Pissaro again, he has thrown out reality, like yourself.

Everard's handkerchief, which has been nestled in Rhoda's bosom, flutters to the ground.

RHODA: Oh!

EVERARD: Allow me.

RHODA: No, I will –

EVERARD: My handkerchief.

RHODA: Oh God.

EVERARD: It gives me hope.

Everard and Rhoda move to a garden area of the exhibition. A gently lit place of colour and possibility.

I have an income – not a large one, but sufficient for us to live, to travel, to study freely.

RHODA: *Never to work again, to see the world with a man on my arm – no, I would be on his arm –*

EVERARD: At first I didn't think of you as a woman – you were interesting because of your mind. Plain, proud, prickly as a briar. Then what was plain began to glow and the pride became delicious, I began to experience your very barbs with a physical thrill. Now your face is lit with a beauty I have rarely seen. It is the one face in all the world I wish to see.

RHODA: *Is it possible? A man, not any man, but an intelligent, well-spoken, well-endowed man with an income loves me – not for beauty or money or position but for myself, for my poor plain soul. Oh, damnable throbbing –*

EVERARD: Rhoda / *Rhoda, Rhoda, Rhoda –*

Everard crushes Rhoda to him.

RHODA: *His manhood pressing against me, the first I've ever felt, I want to sink, swoon, scream!* No!

Rhoda tries to pull away.

Release me.

EVERARD: Release you? Do you mean it? (*still holding her*) Love brings out the savage.

RHODA: Do not use your strength over me!

EVERARD: Women love the feeling of men's strength.

RHODA: Their strength is tyranny!

EVERARD: It is ardour!

RHODA: Domination!

Rhoda breaks away.

All our talk, and you understand nothing of who I am. I am dedicated to a great work.

EVERARD: A free union needn't interfere with your work!

RHODA: Impossible. My work involves not just teaching but *being* an odd woman –

EVERARD: Let someone else sacrifice their life –

RHODA: Showing by example that an unpaired life needn't be a misery, that it can be full of purpose, friends, laughter. Mary is a leader – through my endeavours, so am I. Do you not see the power, the rare power I have found, how it fuels my very being?

EVERARD: Ay. You would be a traitor.

RHODA: I would lose my soul.

EVERARD: Yet it is because you are dedicated to a cause beyond yourself that I admire you the most.

RHODA: *We are lost.*

SCENE 13: THREE VIRGINS AND THE MOON

Mary Barfoot's sitting room.
Late at night.
Alice and Mary have been drinking.
Alice is pounding the type machine ecstatically.

ALICE: I love this machine. I love this machine.

MARY: Thirty words to the minute! Incredible!

ALICE: The precision of it, the sound of it!

MARY: The exultation of the teacher – I haven't felt it in so long. Go on, Alice! Go on! Have some more gin.

ALICE: *I am linked to these keys, to the miraculous pounding, the strength of them opening my mind, I can go more and more quickly and yet not lose the clarity of the print –*

MARY: A spontaneous combustion of learning!

ALICE: (*still typing*) I am beginning to understand the glory of chastity – it isn't the result of not being chosen, a void of negativity, but is part of nature's plan – *If I am happy, I say the unthinkable, that the sex act is not a necessity for everyone, not a necessity for me, I have never yearned as Monica has yearned, but I won't think of Monica, I have been ashamed of the ease of my chastity and now the strength of it pours through me like clear water, like a river in spring!*

MARY: For many women, chastity is more than comfortable –

ALICE: Are you chaste?

MARY: By the letter of the law.

ALICE: Chaste women are the backbone of your movement, yet now these female energies must move towards the earning of money, is that what you believe?

MARY: It is the great flaw in our movement. Women are endlessly, boringly poor.

ALICE: But the world is fuelled by the certain fact that women give. Forgive me, I am on the brink of a thought and it is making all my limbs itch, my arms and my ankles – no, keep the thought – I want tea, cake, gin, itching, I am cold, tired, keep the thought –

MARY: Breathe from the stomach, control your mind –

ALICE: You want to stop us giving and loving for no profit, put a price on caring for a sick animal or a sick parent or the poor –

MARY: Prosperity will bring us freedom.

ALICE: But this returns to love. My constancy, my natural devotion – I am losing it again –

MARY: Your constancy is –

ALICE: Is part of giving with no reward … devotion, love, the idea is coming … yes! I am capable of fearsome feats of devotion, I love objects like this locket, I loved my cat with a gut-wrenching passion, I loved the house we lived in so deeply I felt it part of my skin, I loved my father even though he treated me like an imbecile, Monica, Virginia, I love as I could never love myself. It seems to be in me, in many of us, to love with no reward, and if physical love is a reward, many of the creatures we love longest and most deeply are those we have never even touched. Boundless love, undaunted by ill treatment, abandonment or death. I am showing you love now, by discussing, arguing with you.

MARY: You are making me sing with love.

ALICE: And yet I'm not young and beautiful, like Rhoda.

MARY: I tell her she isn't beautiful.

ALICE: You are wrong.

MARY: Have I ignored you?

ALICE: Yes, but I am old and slow.

MARY: And I am addicted to the young and quick. Forgive me.

ALICE: I was born forgiving people, I forgive curtains and outhouses, slugs and flies, ottomans / and needles –

As a bright moon throws light into the room, Rhoda enters, dressed in a shimmering white nightgown.

RHODA: Ohh, I cannot sleep. I cannot even begin to sleep. Why is no one asleep?

MARY: It's a moony night.

ALICE: She is so enormously full, almost blinding –

RHODA: Why is the moon always 'she'?

ALICE: Three virgins and the moon.

RHODA: Have you been drinking? You have, you're both soused.

ALICE: Here's some of poor Virginia's poison.

Rhoda takes a glass of gin.

Rhoda? There is a flush on you. Has he spoken?

RHODA: No one has spoken.

MARY: Alice is your confidante?

ALICE: Love, hopeless, unflinching love. The gorgeousness of it –

RHODA: I'm thirty-five years old and I've never had words of love spoken to me by a man.

MARY: Are their words so different?

ALICE: Why aren't you happy for her? If I was a woman who yearned, I'd want Everard. Handsome, manly, a bit of a cad –

RHODA: Pass the gin –

MARY: You have had love.

RHODA: A wonderful love.

MARY: Passion.

RHODA: But not –

MARY: Penetration?

ALICE: Mary, I do not believe you are using your intellect –

MARY: Obviously you should accept him.

RHODA: He has not proposed.

MARY: Ha.

RHODA: If he were to propose, which he hasn't, I would not accept him.

ALICE: Not accept him?

RHODA: Of course I wouldn't, but to know that it were possible –

ALICE: If you married you could have children.

RHODA: I could.

MARY: I always wanted a child.

RHODA: You?

MARY: I've seen women driven mad with the lack, but for me, it remains a small, but not overpowering anguish.

ALICE: If only it were possible without the sex act. Perhaps one day –

RHODA: *All I know is that a man held me and I felt a quiver of such exquisite pleasure –*

ALICE: *I ill wish women who have children. I wish them horrible trials, babies with club feet or born with huge bulbous ears, I wish to crush the complacency out of them, the way they say 'my' child – 'my,' 'my,' 'my'!*

MARY: Of course, there would be a financial cost to marrying. The loss of the school, its business, your job and three fine Remingtons.

RHODA: You would disown me?

MARY: Why should I will the school to someone who cannot live up to our principles?

RHODA: Being unmarried is not a principle and never was.

MARY: Fidelity, loyalty are principles.

ALICE: Important principles.

RHODA: But not bondage.

MARY: Bondage! Have I kept / you against your will?

RHODA: No, forgive me, Mary, I am confused / I spoke hastily, never, no, I was confused, I am confused, no, no chains –

MARY: Have I kept you from your separate friends, your own entertainments, locked you in chains? Suddenly I am a great spider, trapping you with filigrees of half-truths. Our conversation has been a god's nectar to us both. Our bodies have known each other, I have licked the crux of you and I have heard you moan my name. Do not let my age wither your reason.

ALICE: Whenever I hold a baby, I fear I'll break into great roaring, howling, gaping sobs, I want to snatch it up, run through the filth of the streets, shrieking, 'I am the real mother!'

MARY: Alice, you are overwrought.

ALICE: Shall we typewrite?

RHODA: We must.

Their passions must find release in the keys.
Alice, Rhoda and Mary move quickly to the Remingtons –

ALICE: *I am alone and the pain is burning, I am alone and the pain is sublime, goading me to new heights / all props are gone, even love, even family –*

MARY: *I am alone and the pain is burning, I am alone and the pain is sublime, goading me to new heights / all props are gone, even love, even family –*

RHODA: *I am alone and the pain is burning, I am alone and the pain is sublime, goading me to new heights / all props are gone, even love, even family –*

ALICE: *Now I soar in my mind, transform myself, though I backslide a thousand times / I will wander in darkness and disarm the light –*

RHODA: *Now I soar in my mind, transform myself, though I backslide a thousand times / I will wander in darkness and disarm the light –*

MARY: *Now I soar in my mind, transform myself, though I backslide a thousand times I will wander in darkness and disarm the light –*

All typing stops.

RHODA: Mary, I desire you no more.

SCENE 14: BERLIN

Days later. Mary's sitting room.
Alice and Mary are typewriting.
Virginia enters and stands in the shadows.
She is bloodied, dressed in a man's suit,
which is ripped and torn.

MARY: Yes? Did you ring the bell?

VIRGINIA: No, I didn't ring. Don't you recognize me?

Virginia sways and almost falls.

MARY: Pardon, I don't … you're bleeding … Virginia?

ALICE: No, it can't be Virginia. *It's someone else, some other poor wrecked creature who's been beaten by navvies, some paltry pinched creature who's stolen men's clothes.*

VIRGINIA: *Alice, Alice forgive me, Alice I've changed, Alice I have been so far, I am altered to the core, yet not altered at all –*

ALICE: *Beast! What have you done with my sister?*

MARY: I'll get bandages. Do we need a doctor? Virginia?

VIRGINIA: No doctor.

Mary exits.

When I arrived after crossing the Channel, there were large men, very large. My attire offended them. They kicked me as if I was a man, but they knew I was a woman – Alice?

ALICE: I'll get you brandy.

VIRGINIA: No. No brandy, that is over.

ALICE: I assume you have a story.

VIRGINIA: I never thought to arrive like this.

ALICE: *Go back, go back to where you came from.*

VIRGINIA: Alice –

ALICE: Here, I can at least wipe your face.

Alice wipes blood away with her handkerchief.

I would do that for a stranger, which is what you are.

VIRGINIA: I wrote.

ALICE: Your cards were very informative: 'Berlin very gloomy, everyone speaks German.' Why not add, 'Dressing like a man. Learning to shave.'?

VIRGINIA: I found such freedom. I learned to whistle. Think of it. Your sister, batty Virginia, walking down the street – no, strolling, swaggering ... ahhhh, my rib is slightly crushed.

ALICE: Swaggering, whistling. Prancing and hopping even.

VIRGINIA: I was very lonely when I first arrived. I lived in a little room not different from our old room, except that you weren't there.

ALICE: No, I was here.

Mary enters with a basin of water and bandages. Mary, and eventually Alice, bandage one of Virginia's wrists and one hand.

VIRGINIA: I am no longer a drunk, does that have no meaning? You liked me when I was dependent, a ditherer, a sodden lump of a brain-soaked body, a body-soaked brain / a great –

MARY: The point is taken. Give me your face.

VIRGINIA: Owww …

MARY: Sit still. *She'll bring attention to us all, parading around in men's duds, who is she to be so brazen?*

ALICE: *My sister is hurt, my sister is bleeding, don't let her be in pain, let me be cut, let me be bruised –*

VIRGINIA: I am healed.

MARY: You are to be congratulated.

ALICE: Bollocks.

VIRGINIA: You have changed.

ALICE: Not as much as you.

VIRGINIA: It's just a suit of clothes.

MARY: *Desire is gone, I am desired no more.*

VIRGINIA: For weeks I stayed alone in that room, a prisoner of nameless terrors, until I realized I had a purse stuffed full of pound notes.

MARY: Of course. You were freed by having money. / It buoyed up your inner resolve.

ALICE: The principal, the principal –

VIRGINIA: I ventured into the city, spending as I went, and began to notice a group of men about the town – they leaned against walls with such panache. One day, I staggered up to them and saw that they were women. They became my friends. They distracted me from my craving, they held me when I shook, they laughed like men but cried like women –

MARY: Did you seek them out because you felt of their kind?

VIRGINIA: May I smoke?

ALICE: I don't care if you set your bum on fire.

MARY: But did you –

VIRGINIA: Did I what?

MARY: *Did you learn what love was, as I learned long ago, before Rhoda, before apprentices and causes.*

Virginia fishes out a package of tobacco and rolling papers from her pocket. As she speaks, she rolls a cigarette but doesn't light it.

VIRGINIA: In no time I had a suit of men's clothes and my hair was shorn. We all went about. Little wants and desires began creeping out of me, like mice seeking the air. To sit in a café, to cross my legs in public, to expound on a topic even though I knew nothing – oh, the wonder of pockets, my hands, being confined, felt freed.

ALICE: But what did you do with these persons?

VIRGINIA: Do?

ALICE: They were deviants.

VIRGINIA: Not at all. The younger ones had beaus, two had children, the others ...

MARY: The others?

VIRGINIA: These were passionate friendships, but friendships they were.

ALICE: Then why did you leave?

MARY: You felt desire.

VIRGINIA: Desire? I'm not certain I would recognize it if I felt it.

MARY: But something frightened you.

VIRGINIA: One night I shared a bed with one of them, which we often did for sisterly economy, but this night she reached for me, I do not know what I felt, will never know, for I began to gasp. I looked down at the locket with Mother and Father's hair intertwined and saw the hair was growing out of the locket 'round my heart, then around my throat, pulling tight, strangling me, Mother and Father and yes, you Alice and Monica were above me calling to me that I had betrayed you and as I lay there I knew it was so. I found myself beating my friend, my hands squeezing, throttling her neck, I nearly killed her. I left on the next train. I return changed but not altered, I have known pockets and cigars, but I am your sister, and our father's daughter still.

ALICE: Are you unnatural or not?

MARY: *She's not unnatural, I am unnatural, shriek it to the skies.*

VIRGINIA: I may never know what I am. But I have been to Berlin. I wish to be a woman, yet dress as a man. Is that so much to ask?

ALICE: Mary, could you allow Virginia to come and go as she is?

MARY: I can be no such rebel. She would draw dangerous attention to the school.

VIRGINIA: Alice, forgive me.

ALICE: Don't you dare! How I wept in despair, how I tore my breast, I don't need you now, blood of my blood –

VIRGINIA: In the name of our dead sisters, of Martha and Isabel –

ALICE: The bonds between women are laughable to the world, but they are marriages in a sense, and they may be betrayed.

MARY: 'Boundless love, undaunted by ill treatment, abandonment or death.' Forgive her, Alice, and take her to your room.

ALICE: Monica said you would own us.

VIRGINIA: Where is Monica?

ALICE: In Hell. Come upstairs, Virginia.

VIRGINIA: Thank you, Mary.

ALICE: Mary be damned. Mary always finds a way to win.

Alice exits. Virginia hangs back, lights her cigarette and has one long, satisfying puff before following Alice to their room.

Mary's sitting room.
Rhoda is fixing a type machine with a great wrench.
Monica enters and watches for a moment.

RHODA: Monica. We see you so rarely now, it seems you come to the house only to change your attire.

MONICA: (*showing her dress*) What do you think?

RHODA: I notice you're wearing a ring. Which 'fiancé' is it now?

MONICA: Let us say I am involved in a free union.

RHODA: Pardon?

MONICA: As a New Woman you should approve.

RHODA: Suddenly, free unions seem common as dirt.

MONICA: *Whip me with your disdain, Rhoda Nunn, and I will gnash my teeth with pleasure.* I was hoping we could have a lesson.

RHODA: A lesson. Why not? Be seated. *She's learned to dress, even though her titties are showing.* Place your hands in position.

MONICA: What position would you like? I can suggest several.

RHODA: One with some dignity.

MONICA: If free unions are undignified and there are no men to marry, then are odd women never to experience passions?

RHODA: I will dictate from this book.

MONICA: We must speak openly of these matters. Erotical silence keeps us all in chains –

RHODA: A demented view of our political ideas.

MONICA: Physically awakened women are a force to be reckoned with – I am beginning to see this power, to know its strength, its reality –

Rhoda isn't listening.

Why have you never liked me? Why?

RHODA: Why should all women be friends with each other? Smiling and cooing and exchanging confidences – *Because the hierarchy of beauty offends me, offends the cause, let us scratch our faces so no woman is more beautiful than the other, receives advantages over the other through an accident of birth, pretty, pretty, born pretty, all your life pretty –*

MONICA: *Let us argue and discuss as you and Mary do, let our minds be kindled –*

RHODA: *She flaunts it, uses it like poppy, like fog.*

MONICA: *The floodgates are open, there is an erotical revolution –*

RHODA: *Everyone assumes you're an old maid because no one wants you and then when they do want you, when they do, you can't believe them –*

MONICA: Some women blaze, we pulse and boil – are you one of us and don't know it? You and I are fertile, soon the time will be gone. I feel myself to be so dreadfully fertile, let me frighten you with what I know. The rubbing and the rocking, then the liquid, filled with babies, boys and girls, dark and fair, running down my legs, some sticking deep inside –

RHODA: Stop, this is a frenzy, a sickness –

Monica is dizzy.

MONICA: *Help me, my body is strange, it feels full of water.*

RHODA: Have you been drinking?

MONICA: A touch of stomach distress.

RHODA: Not the clap?

*The two women stare at each other. The tension is palpable.
Monica breaks the bond and exits.*

SCENE 16: PACKING

*Mary's sitting room.
A spring evening.
Everard and Mary.*

EVERARD: I've never resented the inheritance. Well, not really.

MARY: Then why mention it?

EVERARD: It may be between us.

MARY: That is not what is between us. Do you believe I owe you
something?

EVERARD: Not at all.

MARY: Good.

EVERARD: Be sensible, Mary. Give her up.

MARY: And who am I to say yay or nay?

EVERARD: Don't you see me trembling with the effort of not taking what I choose, of conforming to the ideal of a man who resists the pounding of his own blood? As I resist, my whole body shakes. I was born to be unfair, science tells me that I'm unnatural if I am not savage when I need to be.

MARY: *All my life I have preached the glory of contradiction, yet now my contradictions are repulsive to me, I am caught between waving her farewell or binding her to me with dastardly skills.* You speak of a free union to test her, to see if she's willing to become an outcast for you.

EVERARD: Why shouldn't I test her? She has spoken against love, against marriage, against men – do you think there's no price for those words, that men do not hear them, that we do not wonder and quake?

MARY: I don't give a tinker's damn what she's said. Marry her. Trust her.

EVERARD: I must know her true feelings. If she truly is a New Woman, she must find marriage abhorrent and accept a free union. If she accepts the free union, she proves both her politics and her love for me. Then I will, of course, marry her.

MARY: Why men call women's logic impaired, I will never know.

Rhoda enters.

RHODA: Everard.

EVERARD: Rhoda. I hear you're taking your holidays.

RHODA: I leave tomorrow for the Lake Country.

EVERARD: I'll be in the area myself. We could meet, have a day's ramble together.

RHODA: The Lake Country is free to you.

EVERARD: I'll stay in Seascale, at a small inn called the Traveller.

RHODA: I can't promise to be at any one particular spot – we may meet, by chance. By merely walking about, as we'll be in the same area, at the same time, as the lush spring unfolds, as the animals are pawing and mating. I must go. Pack.

EVERARD: I will hope to meet up with you. Until then –

RHODA: Until then –

EVERARD: (as he exits) Mary.

RHODA: *I am softer now, I feel that I am softer. Can you see it?*

MARY: *I am blind at the moment.*

RHODA: *My shoulders melt instead of stiffen in a crisis, my breastbone yields. Tell me you see it –*

MARY: *Forgive me. I wanted to keep you as a talisman against death.*

RHODA: *You let him into our lives, you handed him to me –*

MARY: *Perhaps I did, but you didn't have to take him.*

RHODA: *A test? A trick? Be sweet, Mary –*

MARY: *Why sweet? Mary Barfoot who has spit and smashed is now meek and humble?*

RHODA: *Smash me and make me whole again. I am so afraid.*

Mary touches Rhoda on the cheek.

MARY: Never be afraid. May these holidays be all that you wish them to be.

Mary exits.

SCENE 17: SEASCALE

A grassy hilltop overlooking the sea.
Bright sunshine. Birds twitter.
Everard and Rhoda loll on a picnic blanket.

EVERARD: *A perfect day, yet everything is in the balance –*

RHODA: *If I'm about to burst into flower, then let it happen –*

EVERARD: I think we should live in that cottage for six months, then take the Orient Express to the Bosphorus, winter in Florence –

RHODA: We'd be so tired of each other by then.

EVERARD: Shhh, the day is perfect. We'd be endlessly enchanted and inspired. Tomorrow we go to Coniston.

RHODA: We?

EVERARD: We. Yes. Rhoda –

Rhoda and Everard lunge at each other's mouths, fall backwards onto the blanket, thrashing, running their hands over each other's bodies. In a moment of true heroism, Everard drags himself away.

We must speak. Mary / is …

RHODA: Is a wise woman.

Everard and Rhoda resume kissing, touching, panting, exploring passionately.

EVERARD: I have longed to speak freely of my love.

RHODA: But what is your love worth?

EVERARD: In pounds? Four hundred a year. In constancy ...

Rhoda drags herself away.

RHODA: Wait! *Bargain, I must bargain for my life –*

EVERARD: *And so it begins, with my balls aching and my strength rising, how not to be a barbarian?*

RHODA: Is there any woman living who has a claim on you?

EVERARD: No promise of love exists between myself and any woman.

RHODA: I would deeply resent unfaithfulness.

EVERARD: That is the understanding between man and wife.

Everard and Rhoda lunge together again.
Rhoda pulls away quickly.

RHODA: But what do you mean by 'man and wife'?

EVERARD: I mean we would be 'as' man and wife.

RHODA: But not?

EVERARD: You have often said, 'Any woman who reads the marriage contract and still gets married ...' However it goes –

RHODA: Don't trap me with my own words – *I announce that I have refused marriage, live openly with a man, how noble, how emancipated –*

EVERARD: Your ideals will be protected. Even if you teach no more.

RHODA: *Teach no more – but without a public promise, I could be abandoned without a thought –*

EVERARD: *Prove your love, Rhoda, prove your love –*

RHODA: It's no small thing to be an outcast – are you prepared to lose family, friends, all but the few who would accept us?

EVERARD: If we think of ourselves as married, we are married. I don't need to convert the world.

Rhoda and Everard kiss and grope with even greater urgency. Everard puts his hand up Rhoda's skirt. We see a flash of lace.

RHODA: Then we would merely say that we are married? That is not an ideal, it's deception.

Everard pulls away.

EVERARD: Do you doubt your own love?

RHODA: I do not doubt it. In spite of all my efforts, I love you, Everard Barfoot. I love the struggle I see in you, I love your intellect, I love your physical self.

EVERARD: Then give me your left hand.

Everard slips a ring on Rhoda's marriage finger.

RHODA: What –

EVERARD: We'd wear rings for certain circumstances, / they can be bought readily and …

RHODA: No! Horrible, take it off, it's burning me, it's a lie, we would be liars, neither heroic nor conventional, / this proves to me I cannot pretend. Take it back or I'll drop it in the sand!

EVERARD: We would use it merely for convention, if we were travelling for instance, for hotels and trains, for relatives abroad – it's merely a ring.

RHODA: More than a ring. Dearest, Everard dearest –

EVERARD: *Oh God, the iron fist in the velvet glove.* Say it once more.

RHODA: Dearest – *See how well I do it, like any woman / like an ordinary woman with all her wretched wiles –*

EVERARD: *She's like an ordinary woman asking for ordinary things* – You want that old idle form?

RHODA: I find that I do.

EVERARD: *Who is she?* We can get a licence from the registrar and be married in that little … church.

RHODA: Church?

EVERARD: Grove? Mud hut? Pub?

RHODA: If it must be a church –

EVERARD: Then I am resigned.

RHODA: Resigned?

EVERARD: Ecstatic.

RHODA: *He is disappointed, he has changed* – Do you love me any the less? *Weak, simpering girl* –

EVERARD: Come here. *Do I love her less?* Let me dominate you in this at least.

They kiss, but less passionately than before.

EVERARD: I have been weak.

RHODA: Yielding in the one point that didn't matter to you at all?

EVERARD: Yielding at the very beginning of the war.

RHODA: There's someone coming.

EVERARD: It's the boy from the hotel. He's waving a letter.

RHODA: I feel faint.

Rhoda and Everard remain onstage during the next scene.

SCENE 18: INFIDELITY

Mary's sitting room.
Alice has called a meeting.
Mary, Virginia, Alice and Monica.
Virginia is dressed in women's clothing.

ALICE: Monica is pregnant and we believe the father is Everard Barfoot.

MARY: What? / No, oh no –

ALICE: He used Monica to sate his desire while he waited patiently for Rhoda.

MARY: You've been intimate with him? Monica?

ALICE: This is the future, emancipated women claiming their bodies in order to frig as many men as they possibly can.

MARY: That is not what emancipation / signifies.

ALICE: Monica told me she was engaged.

VIRGINIA: Fanciful manias – that she was engaged, yet every man she introduced you to was different? You closed your eyes, sister.

MARY: Monica needs your pity and your help.

VIRGINIA: What does it matter? Our dear little girl will give us a child. Forget marriage, let us care for it –

ALICE: A bastard. What life would it have?

MONICA: Stupid Everard and stupid stupid Rhoda!

MARY: What do you know about Rhoda?

MONICA: He talked to me about her, how he was going to get her to bed without marriage just to prove she was like any other woman – *She is free and I am trapped, as all women are trapped by the very nature of our bodies, I hate my body, I hate it!*

MARY: She is in the country now, with Everard.

ALICE: You must warn her.

MARY: But is the child Everard's? Monica, do you hear me? A woman's future is at stake.

MONICA: I used a reproductive pamphlet I found in this house, counted the days – the pamphlets are wrong, we are ignorant, left to the mercy of creation which damns all our hopes!

ALICE: Mary, you must write Rhoda. She is about to marry the man who must now marry Monica.

MARY: Monica? Is it that you don't know who the father is?

ALICE: / Oh God.

MARY: Do you know? Then who is it?

VIRGINIA: Why won't you speak?

ALICE: It is Everard's.

MARY: Rhoda will hate me forever if I am the one to tell her.

ALICE: She'll hate you more if she knows you didn't warn her. You must write her now, before she accepts him.

MARY: Monica, is this true? Monica? I swear to heaven, if I were a man I'd beat it out of you!

ALICE: You / will do no such thing.

VIRGINIA: Touch one hair on her head –

MONICA: Go to hell. All of you, be cursed as I am cursed!

Monica runs out of the room.

MARY: It is all ruined. Why did I let you in? Why did I let any of you in?

Mary exits.
Alice opens a notebook.

ALICE: (*writing*) 'Dear Rhoda, I must inform you of a matter of a desperate and urgent nature …'

The grassy hilltop.
Rhoda holds Alice's letter in her hand.

EVERARD: I have told you it isn't true! Why won't you believe me?

RHODA: Then what is the explanation?

EVERARD: I have none.

RHODA: You refuse to explain?

EVERARD: I will not. You must trust me.

RHODA: I cannot offer blind trust!

EVERARD: When you are prepared to take my word, you know where to find me.

SCENE 19: ALONE

Five months later.
A dull afternoon.
Mary's sitting room.
Rhoda and Monica.
Monica is seven months pregnant.

MONICA: It's taken me many months to find the courage to see you.

RHODA: Five. Five months to be exact.

MONICA: I am going to die.

RHODA: Such a loss.

MONICA: When he heard what was said, how did Everard respond?

RHODA: You know that he denied it. He was above explanations. We haven't spoken since that day.

MONICA: Not a word in five months? No wonder you look so drawn and liverish.

RHODA: And you look like a wraith who's swallowed a balloon.

MONICA: It wasn't him. It wasn't Everard.

RHODA: Why should I believe anything you say?

MONICA: We did explore the amatory act on a number of pleasant occasions, but long before. The man whose child this is abandoned me. You saw him at the exhibition. He's wealthy and a shite.

RHODA: So you did lie with Everard.

MONICA: It's not Everard's. You ruined everything. You couldn't just love him, you couldn't just trust him.

RHODA: Then why didn't you speak at the time? Do you hate me that much?

MONICA: You were about to leave us all behind.

RHODA: Why are you speaking now?

MONICA: I felt it move.

RHODA: Felt it move?

MONICA: And I needed money from the real father. I've hated it all this time, and / now –

RHODA: And now you love it. You felt it move.

MONICA: I feel nothing for it. But it is moving, like a fish in its watery bowl. Before I die, it deserves the truth.

RHODA: All new mothers believe they're going to die.

MONICA: My sisters are taking care of me and the man has sent money so he isn't even a complete villain. But I am so weary. I can feel the child wanting hope, sucking, searching for it, and I have none. It is as if all I believed in was a lie.

RHODA: No. It isn't.

MONICA: I always felt that you had something to give me, that you could help –

RHODA: Are you shaming me? I should be ashamed. I have always been a jealous person.

MONICA: And I've been green with envy – I'll get out my whip and flay us both. Tell me about the future.

RHODA: The future? That tired old horse? Oh God, but I'm weary too.

MONICA: But you believe.

RHODA: Yes. We live for the future. You must live for the future.

MONICA: I cannot. I fear I will die with this newness inside me, struggling to be born.

RHODA: This is defeat. And I won't have it. I am able to stop these thoughts with my will, can you feel my will?

MONICA: It's like a ray of cold steel.

RHODA: Then I'll warm the metal. Think. Feel. Every breath you take, you are breathing the future. The reddest blood must flow to it, the strongest muscle, your heart, must pound for the child. Hear its rhythm, feel its pulse. Let it be a drum that drowns out weakness, that dwells on life, as we must. As we must.

MONICA: As we must. Yes. We could have been friends.

RHODA: Yes.

MONICA: Goodbye, Rhoda.

RHODA: Not goodbye.

MONICA: It is a shame that sex matters are so … untidy.

Monica exits.
Everard rushes in.

EVERARD: *You stubborn cow –*

RHODA: *You could have told me –*

EVERARD: *You look older and your dress is out of style –*

RHODA: *I didn't quite believe you –*

EVERARD: *I've been travelling for months –*

RHODA: *There have been casualties for the cause –*

EVERARD: *Paris, Florence, the beauty of the frescoes –*

RHODA: *Two suicides, one genteel starvation –*

EVERARD: *It wasn't true, I wasn't pure, but I wasn't –*

RHODA: *I know, I know –*

EVERARD: *I am a magician, I wave my wand and take us back to that day in Seascale, the sun sparkles, the grass is green, I ask you to marry me –*

RHODA: *That is not what you asked –*

EVERARD: *It was a good offer, an excellent offer –*

RHODA: Neither of us was happy –

EVERARD: DO NOT TOY WITH ME! I ask for the last time, will you marry me?

RHODA: *This is the man for me, made and unmade for me* – I am not a very rapid typist. If you typewrite at high speeds, there comes a time when you can't comprehend the words, you must surrender to the physical movement and become an automaton. When this occurs, I always become afraid. I deliberately stop, even stumble, so that my brain will catch up and I am able to understand. There is wonder in the surrender and pain in the stopping, but only then am I fully conscious. I will always remember that day.

EVERARD: Rhoda. Even now ...

RHODA: Even now, I have just enough courage left to send you on your way.

Everard bows his head to Rhoda and exits.

SCENE 20: THE GARDEN

Three months later.
Bright sunlight floods a garden outside a country house.
Alice is holding a baby.
Mary sits beside her.
Virginia behind them, dashingly dressed in men's clothing.

MARY: Alice, I have never seen you looking so well.

ALICE: Yes, she definitely agrees with me. (*to baby*) Don't you, little Monica? Yes, yes you do.

VIRGINIA: She is always hungry.

ALICE: I love to watch her eyes as she drinks. They stare at me with such an expression.

VIRGINIA: Greed.

ALICE: Stop it.

VIRGINIA: It is a greed for life.

MARY: Rather than greed, call it lust.

ALICE: Lust? This poor little creature?

VIRGINIA: I've got a such a lust for a pint of gin. The only way I can keep off the bottle is to dress like a man. It fortifies me in a very deep and superficial way.

ALICE: But only within the home.

VIRGINIA: My rebellion is contained but not obliterated. I long to see Berlin again –

ALICE: Not yet, dear.

VIRGINIA: No dear, not yet.

Rhoda enters.

RHODA: The house is lovely.

ALICE: Paid for by little Monica's father. He's been very good, really. It's the old kind of commerce. I give you a baby, die, and you support it and my two sisters. Once she's older, we'll finally become business women and open a school for young children. We'll call it Day Time Care.

MARY: Brilliant.

VIRGINIA: Let me take her.

ALICE: I would prefer to hold her.

VIRGINIA: You must be tired.

ALICE: I'm not tired.

VIRGINIA: She's about to cry.

ALICE: She is smiling.

MARY: May I hold her?

ALICE: She's very heavy.

MARY: I have muscles of iron.

ALICE: If you insist.

MARY: Yes, yes, little one. Sqoodgy woodgy woodgy ... she is smiling.

RHODA: I enjoy watching other people hold babies.

ALICE: Do you see Everard? I mean, as friends?

RHODA: Not often.

VIRGINIA: Is it true he's married?

RHODA: Her father is quite wealthy, but I hear she's an intelligent girl. For a trollop.

MARY: She has her mother's light bright eyes. Monica's funeral was the saddest I've ever attended.

RHODA: It was gut-wrenching.

ALICE: I thought some of the men she serviced could have come.

VIRGINIA: There were a few. Now I will hold her.

MARY: Very well.

Mary passes the baby to Virginia.

ALICE: Our poor dear had a terrible time. At the end, it seemed the baby would never be born, but then Monica rallied, swore like a sailor, gave a great push and little Monica was born.

VIRGINIA: She was very brave.

RHODA: More than brave.

MARY: A casualty of the war.

Pause.

RHODA: (*leaning over the baby*) It's as if she's thinking of something astonishing.

VIRGINIA: She's soiling her nappy.

ALICE: I wonder if she'll learn to typewrite.

MARY: She won't have to typewrite.

RHODA: Now I would like to hold her.

Virginia passes the baby to Rhoda.

VIRGINIA: Mind her neck.

RHODA: I am minding her neck.

VIRGINIA: And her little foot.

ALICE: You look a little stiff.

RHODA: I am capable of holding an infant.

ALICE: Does your heart melt?

RHODA: Not quite.

VIRGINIA: And your work?

MARY: Flourishing. Of course, Rhoda's taken over a great deal of the daily duties while I travel the world giving speeches.

ALICE: So you won. You have your apprentice after all.

MARY: Rhoda is no longer an apprentice but a business partner. She now owns half of our enterprise.

VIRGINIA: Equals?

RHODA: Perhaps.

VIRGINIA: *Lovers?*

RHODA: *No longer.* We're doing so well, we have to purchase a larger building. And we are beginning a women's publishing house.

MARY: The first in London.

RHODA: People keep suggesting martyred titles like Crucible Press. But I think it should say something about freedom.

ALICE: She looks irritable.

RHODA: She's very happy at the moment.

ALICE: I will hold her.

RHODA: Soon.

VIRGINIA: Is she asleep?

RHODA: Not yet.

ALICE: I'm so glad it was a girl.

VIRGINIA: Are you?

RHODA: The fire has been lit, it is burning through society with ferocious speed, no household is safe, the world is moving. (*to the baby*) In thirty years, it will all be accomplished.

They form a loose tableau.
The lights dim very slowly,
Until finally,
The women disappear.

CURTAIN

A FLAGRANTLY WEIRD AGE

A reaction to research, time travel and
the history of the suffragettes

In *Age of Arousal*, time is collapsed, inverted, stomped on, in an effort to straddle important points in Britain's struggle for women's rights. It's all true, just rearranged. The play is set in 1885. The time period that encompasses all aspects of the play is from 1869 to 1914. Forty-five years.

I wanted the play set in deep Victoriana, influenced by the Married Women's Property Act of 1870, as well as by the militant feminist movement, which arguably began with the first arrest in 1905. Why 1885? I wanted the fusty velvets, the tight corsets, the claustrophobia of a world about to ignite. I wanted a blast of modernity to come from underneath the dust bunnies of Victorian England. I wanted the play to reflect the population imbalance that was registered in the late 1880s and was the impetus for George Gissing's novel, *The Odd Women*. I wanted the feel of a time that did not have the First World War hovering over it, although it's possible that this atmosphere helped to produce the militant women's movement. I wanted women's violence – educated ladies of the middle and upper classes jailed with rats, shitting into buckets, smashing windows, setting fire to buildings, destroying delicate orchids. Women by the hundreds thrown into prison and tortured.

In spite of the irreverence towards linear time in *Age of Arousal*, the real issues and human contradictions of the women's suffrage movement (and its modern equivalents) form the ideological bedrock of the play. To narrowly define the suffrage movement is to demean it. Women fought for more than the right to vote – they fought for legal, social and psychological liberation. As Susan Kingsley Kent, in *Sex and Suffrage in Britain*, a main source during the writing of this play, says, 'In fighting for enfranchisement, suffragists sought no less than the total transformation of the lives of women. They set out to redefine and recreate, by political means, the sexual culture of Britain.'[1] I'm not an academic, and there are countless books on both the Victorian age and Britain's suffrage movement, but I wanted to give a sense of what I discovered, of what was meaningful to me, as well as an accurate timeline of events. Mighty people were involved, with awesome energy and an almost biblical sense of commitment. My concentration on the sexual lives of the women in *Age of Arousal* is part of a continuing exploration of the relationship between sex, politics and emotions.

I was concerned with a certain world, a certain time. The fact that women in all societies, of all races, have fought and do fight with grit and dedication for the cause of women's emancipation has to be acknowledged. As you read this, women and men of incalculable spirit bleed for the future.

RESEARCH AND TIME

I didn't research in an academic way. I'd read a serious book of facts and dates, then curl up with a Jane Austen DVD, even though those take place in the 1830s. I luxuriated to Johnny Depp's version of J. M. Barrie in the film *Neverland*. I reread George Eliot, D. H. Lawrence, Thomas Hardy, Henry James, Edith Wharton. It was the most delicious time travel. I've always been a bit of a Merchant-Ivory slut, dreaming my way through many hours of perfectly produced costume drama – but I felt guilty at the same time. The lack of edge, the sometimes saccharine devotion to form. No matter how well these dramas serve the original authors, it's hard to get a sense of the groundbreaking nature of their work through the mists of time. It all looks so … acceptable. I was determined that *Age of Arousal* would blast past reverence into new territory.

In an effort to understand the women's movement of the late nineteenth and early twentieth centuries, I began to read 'first-wave' modern feminists for the first time – I'd never read Germaine Greer, Kate Millett or Betty Freidan. What was startling was the similarity of the thinking, the similarity of the issues, the similarity of the fight.

Above all, I saw that the suffragettes were frighteningly contemporary.

The fact that social and political 'progress' doesn't move neatly forwards was vividly brought home to me as I began this research. I felt trapped in the space/time continuum of science fiction, watching legal and social realizations go backwards, forwards and backwards again. Women's rights wiggled around. The awareness of women's issues was much higher in 1912 than in the 1950s. In terms of the vote, rights that had existed were literally taken away – a single woman in Britain who owned property was able to vote, until the Reform Law of 1832 revoked that right (although married women had never been allowed to vote). I was following the ongoing evolution of European democracy, moving away from aristocratic rule towards an increased voice for the middle class. The *male* middle class. In 1832, for the first time in Britain's history, the word 'male' was inserted before 'persons' (foretelling the Persons case in Canada in 1929) and, with the stroke of a quill, women were disenfranchised. The new law applied only to those who wore pants and had money. Women suddenly joined criminals, paupers and the insane as non-voting members of society.

If there is one date that signifies the official beginning of the European fight for women's rights, it's much earlier than 1869, when I chose to begin my timeline. When I first read Mary Wollstonecraft's *A Vindication of the Rights of Women*, I cried. First published in 1792, it's a more complete and far-reaching treatise than appeared anywhere during the weird 1950s. I tried to imagine this woman, so isolated, so unusual, reaching forwards and backwards in time to articulate what women have known since the Garden of Eden. Her extraordinary mind dealt with women's rights in the context of human rights:

> It is vain to expect virtue from women till they are in some degree independent of men; nay, it is vain to expect that strength of natural affection which would make them good wives and mothers. Whilst they are absolutely dependent on their husbands they will be cunning, mean, and selfish; and the men who can be gratified by the fawning fondness of spaniel-like affection have not much delicacy, for love is not to be bought; in any sense of the words, its silken wings are instantly shrivelled up when anything beside a return in kind is sought. Yet whilst wealth enervates men, and women live, as it were, by their personal charms, how can we expect them to discharge those ennobling duties which equally require exertion and self-denial?[2]

'Victorian' has become synonymous with 'sexless,' 'repressed,' 'joyless.' Yet we read about them voraciously, they populate our TV sets, fashion returns to them again and again. We love the Victorians. They are our most recent ancestors. And if we believe that humans are humans, no matter what the time period, then their sexuality has to be there, somewhere. We know that there were more prostitutes per capita in London during the 1890s than at any other time in history. We know there was an abundance of pornography, that venereal disease was close to epidemic. Contrary to what we traditionally assume, the Victorians were sex-obsessed, or at least the men were. And new opinions, like those of Peter Gay (*Schnitzler's Century*), reveal much less horror and much more sexual enjoyment on the part of Victorian women than we imagine. During this age, both men and women were caught in a dynamic struggle between the pull of Eros, the scepticism of the age and the teachings of societal respectability. This was a fertile, combustible time, so different from the cliché of dull prudishness. The polarized contrast of thought and language, of inner desire and outward behaviour, makes the Victorians irresistible.

This was a time of great belief in the future. I began to see the Victorians as optimists – they believed the world was going to be figured out. Darwin was the controversial king, and it was just a matter of time before all aspects of the human condition would be understood and, more importantly, resolved. Victorians were intent on improving themselves and their environment. They had a great faith that all would be fixed, and soon. I realized that everything we are dealing with now – the rise of technology, bureaucracy, women's issues, men's issues, capitalism vs. communism vs. socialism, atheism, the fascination with psychology, the triumph of science in every realm – began in this period. It was the past and it is the future.

'[Women] operate by personal influence, and not by associated or representative action ... [T]heir natural sphere is not the turmoil and dust of politics, but the circle of social and domestic life,'[3] said Prime Minister H. H. Asquith (1900–1916), arch-enemy of women's suffrage.

Victorians believed in the concept of 'separate spheres.' Men belonged in the public sphere, women in the private sphere. The separate-sphere theory had its roots in the belief that women's function in having children meant they were incapable of logic, reasoning and higher intellectual functions. If a woman concentrated on her brain, her ovaries would wither. The Victorian delight in science supported this belief, and the medical profession gave it the air of absolute scientific fact.

The division between male and female in the nineteenth century has a nastily familiar sound to it. Men inhabited the world of reason, action, aggression, independence and self-interest. Women's qualities were emotion, passivity, submission, dependence and selflessness, all of which came automatically from her biological capacities.[4] These beliefs, treated as facts, contributed to the separate-sphere theory. The fact that working-class women had laboured in factories since the beginning of the Industrial Revolution was considered a sad state of affairs brought on not by their ability to thrive in the workplace but by economic necessity. This created a natural connection between the women's movement and the Independent Labour Party. Still, most women and men, from every class believed that women were physiologically incapable of comprehending the issues of the day.

WOMANLY GRACES

The Victorians believed that women had achieved a preferred status in society, a gilded pedestal from which they watched the sordid doings of the male world. Victorian women had been elevated to the position of 'angel of the home.' Imagine beautiful drawings of women in ringlets and regalia, a hint of wings, bending over the crib of a chubby child. Women's natural delicacy and refinement (the working classes were excluded – not refined enough, not delicate enough) meant that voting would be a coarsening influence. More than that, they would lose their identity as women. This foreshadows the early 1970s, when it was believed that if women were to truly compete in the corporate world they would need to 'become men.' At the turn of the century, as in the 1970s, there was a need to fight for equality of opportunity. But reducing the complexity of the sexes to a slogan called 'equality' has its dangers. As Germaine Greer articulates, the goal of equality is limiting – a larger vision is to 'endow our differences with dignity and prestige.'[5] The battle for women's suffrage was also a larger struggle – a battle to include the individual qualities of women and men into a new world vision.

In the Victorian era, a woman's purity was considered both innate and easily destroyed. A woman's influence in the private sphere was considered to be equal or greater than a man's, even though it took place in the home. William Gladstone, the grand prime minister of the 1880s, had a wonderful way of stating what many people believed about giving women the right to vote: 'The fear I have … is lest we should invite her unwittingly to trespass upon the delicacy, the purity, the refinement, the elevation of her own nature, which are the present sources of its power.'[6]

Angel of the home, all-powerful, all pure. Woman's purity was also a societal construct to protect her from herself. It was believed by many that if the velvet chains were released from her delicate wrists, hell would break loose. Because women were ultimately physical, they were like nature itself – unpredictable, unreasonable, dangerous. Women's passions, once unleashed, would be uncontainable, given that reason had no place in her nature. Without legal and societal boundaries, she might become sexually voracious.

Here things get beautifully contradictory. At the same time as they were potential tsunamis of desire, women were considered sexually passionless. Back to pure and refined. Maybe the idea was that if they stayed in the private sphere, having children and influencing from within, women's sexuality was happily, even naturally dormant. But there was an even more ornate twist to the logic. Defining women entirely as a reproductive/sexual being reached a new level in this age – they began to be referred to simply as 'The Sex.' This term held all kinds of opportunities for degradation. Woman as animal, passionless but defined purely by sex function. Kent says, 'This collapsing of sex and gender – the physiological facts with the normative social creation – made it possible for women to be construed as at once both pure and purely sexual.'[7] Women became pure bodies. Why would bodies want rights and freedoms? They were The Sex – if they protested, they were unsexed. But they weren't supposed to like sex, unless they were unleashed, and then who knew what might happen.

SEX WAR

Anti-suffragists were afraid that the rights and freedoms women demanded would lead to a disintegration of family life. A wife might no longer legally and emotionally acquiesce to her husband. She might engage with men in the workplace, where liaisons could develop. If women spoke up in the home, had an equal say in everything from their children's education to family finances, a constant, unrelenting Sex War would be created, sabotaging any hope for peace and stability. Women would be placed in direct competition and rivalry with men. Two opposite poles pitted against each other without end. War.

If there was one argument of the female anti-suffragists that made me pause, it was that women were placing themselves in terrible danger by engaging in the Sex War. Coming from a different place than the conventional female viewpoint that it was better to serve quietly from the shadows, it had an air of real fear, of cynicism about the male species. It was assumed that women would lose the Sex War and, in fighting, would shatter a balance that had protected them from men. They believed that men were inherently brutal, that women had a civilizing effect on this brutality as long as they didn't confront men outside of the protected sphere where they secretly held sway. He was stronger, louder, more aggressive and more sexually driven. If chivalry disappeared, what was to keep him from imposing his will more often and more violently? In this we find a deep pessimism about our inherent natures, about nature itself. Women cooled the violent eruptions of the male beast, but only by indirect means. The minute they chose to challenge, their influence disappeared. It was women's inherent weakness, her 'inspired unfitness', that not only gave her a secret strength but protected all of society. Her very weakness served to appeal to man's best nature. Without her weakness, what would hold men back?

It made a dreadful kind of sense. There are no statistics on domestic violence for this age, no way to find out if it increased with the growth of women's rights, but even to entertain the idea is disturbing. Victorian feminists were optimists, believing that negative gender traits were learned and therefore could be changed. Anti-suffragists believed these traits were genetic and would only get worse with confrontation. At the time, Olive Katherine Parr stated, 'Our judges complain that crimes of violence on women are becoming more common. Little children, lonely women are brutally done to death. This horror will increase as more women claim equality with men and deny his protectorship.'[8]

The use of 'sex' in Sex War doesn't just refer to gender but includes the act itself. If women had a say in the home, in all aspects of their lives, if women's sexual drive was less than men's, would they ever have sex with their husbands? Would children ever be born? Men would be penalized, as their sexual rapaciousness was innate. 'Not tonight, dear, I have a headache' would be replaced by 'I don't want to tonight.' Rape was rarely mentioned but was alluded to, one anti-feminist stating flatly, 'Sex-lawlessness … is an innate Male-trait.'[9] The connection between women having a say in whether or not they had sex, and aberrant, dangerous behaviour was being made by doctors as early as 1875.

The fact that women were legislated to have sex with their husbands and were often totally ignorant on their wedding night may have contributed to a lack of enthusiasm. There was a confusion in the women's movement at the time, and even to some extent during the feminist wave of the 1970s, as to whether sex with men was a good thing or not. Did it mean subjugation to men or could it mean women claiming their bodies as objects of their own pleasure as well as another's? 'Born to breed' was not an attractive way to live one's life. If women merely traded their sexual favours and child-bearing capacities for room and board, then they weren't much different from prostitutes – they just got paid less.

MARRIAGE

Reading about marriage in the nineteenth century can help to explain the tendrils of subjugation that even now can strangle the moment of promise. It's the legalities that are so appalling. But again, the guiding principles of the Victorian age aren't the moribund ideas we imagine. The Victorian age was about change. Women and men were fighting to loosen many chains, among these the rules of bondage that made up the marriage contract. This happened in stages, from the first property challenges in 1830 to 1925, when mothers were finally given guardianship of their children upon the death of the father.

The following situation still existed in 1869 and continued, with adjustments, until the 1900s: under the law, married women had no rights or existence apart from their husbands. The legal existence of a married woman was suspended, or at least incorporated into that of the husband, who was supposed to protect her. A married woman had no legal rights to her property or her earnings, no freedom of movement. This was amended to some extent in 1870, when women were allowed to keep their own earnings, and was amended again in 1886. Before this, upon marriage, a woman's assets automatically became the property of her husband. A woman could watch her dowry and future financial stability spent on mistresses and gambling with no legal redress. Until 1886, the husband was given complete authority over her children – where they lived, their schooling, their religion, their guardianship after his death. Her physical body was 'under the protection' of her husband. Even though this law was rarely used, up until 1884 husbands could have their wives jailed if they refused to have sex with them, even if the men were diseased or violent.

Feminists charged that the legal right of husbands to force sexual intercourse and compulsory child-bearing amounted to 'sex slavery'. No surprise that this influenced women's feelings about sex, bringing about a sense that men's sexuality was a brute force, keeping them in a state of legal marital rape. Elizabeth Wolstenholme Elmy wrote, 'The only absolute right I should claim for a woman as against a man … is that she should never be made a mother against her will.'[10]

Love, affection and true passion, was of course, present in marriages of the age no matter what the legalities. A tender tidbit of Victorian intimacy appears in Peter Gay's *Shnitzler's Century*: an account of William Gladstone 'gently, piously, stroking his wife's breasts to alleviate a stoppage that kept her from breast-feeding her infant.'[11]

These are our ancestors. These long-forgotten laws continue to have an impact on us. Behaviours and beliefs echo for generations after, reverberating into the perfect condos of young married couples, sneaking into the air systems of family homes, polluting the atmosphere as we all attempt the oh-so-delicate balance of love, sex and the outside world.

SPINSTERS

Then there were the spinsters, hundreds of thousands of them. By the 1851 census there were 405,000 more women than men in Britain. By 1885, the number was even higher, some saying there were half a million more women than men in London alone. Sheila Jeffreys calculates that 'In the late Victorian period, almost one in three of all adult women were single and one in four would never marry.'[12]

These numbers have been questioned, but no scholar denies that the problem of 'excess' or 'surplus' women caused great alarm among male commentators. These women weren't servicing men or breeding, so what was their purpose? Spinsters were treated with contempt, and there was a drive to send them all to America, where there were hundreds of thousands of single men. One article on the subject even calculated the number of ships it would take to offload the entire population of spinsters to the New World – 10,000 ships would have to make 10,000 voyages.[13]

Middle-class spinsters were in the worst situation, as their background hadn't prepared them to earn a living, unlike the women of the working classes. Domestic servants were almost entirely spinster women, so at least working-class women had a way to survive and the companionship of others. But the poor faded flowers of the middle classes, bred to weakness and submission, were entirely unsuited for a world in which they must support themselves, and they were denied entry into many areas of employment. Yes, they could have taken up a mop themselves but, given the class system in Britain, that would never do. Trapped, celibate, penniless, living with married relatives, their lives must have seemed an untold misery. But the feminist movement created a new kind of spinster – active, educated, even choosing to remain celibate. Some considered spinsterhood a political decision, a deliberate choice made in response to the conditions of sex slavery. The refusal of marriage and motherhood came to be seen as a 'silent strike' against the conditions of both.

Once a single life was accepted, or even chosen, new kinds of relationships developed between women who were no longer seen as competitors for the same small pool of men. The cat fight was replaced by cat power. The new spinsters experienced solidarity, embraced their chastity and flocked to the feminist cause, forming the backbone of the new feminist movement. They were suddenly a force to be reckoned with. The spinsters who didn't embrace chastity were faced with new choices – sexual freedoms have been part of all revolutionary eras, and this was no different. Many of those women who found chastity, even as a robust active choice, to be unsatisfying, explored their sexuality, taking enormous chances, determined to find a way for their sexual selves to be a part of an expanding consciousness.

SAPPHIC VICTORIANS

Queen Victoria believed there was no such thing as sexual love between women. It was so unthinkable it wasn't even against the law. Oscar Wilde was tried and jailed for something called 'sodomy' but there was no official language to describe such an act between women. Sarah Waters, in her novel *Tipping the Velvet*, uses 'toms' to describe gay women. It may be that the streets of London offered a number of other juicy labels for the impossible sin. The women of the suffrage movement were called everything under the sun, including 'deviant', 'unnatural' and whatever else the walls of Victorian toilets could come up with.

Yet it seems inconceivable that there were no lesbian relationships in a movement dominated by thousands of women. In Victorian England, women had passionate friendships, many without a sexual content, but the intensity often seems highly romantic. Academic Lillian Faderman argues that

> These romantic friendships were love relationships in every sense except perhaps the genital … since women in centuries other than ours often internalized the view of females as having little sexual passion. Thus they might kiss, fondle each other, sleep together, utter expressions of overwhelming love and promises of eternal faithfulness, and yet see their passions as nothing more than effusions of the spirit. If they were sexually aroused, bearing no burden of visible truth as men do, they might deny it even to themselves if they wished.[14]

The upshot is, yes, there were gay women in Victorian England as there have been gay women throughout history, but many of the women themselves may have been unaware of what they were doing. They didn't call it anything. Maybe 'cuddling'.

Men were sent to jail for deviant sexual behaviour, but women were much more likely to be sent to an insane asylum. The behaviour was seen as pathological, and physicians defined lesbianism as an illness caused by 'cerebral abnormalities'. With men it was criminal, with women it was sick. Again, we see the long arm of science and its practical partners, the doctors, creating a view that for women to initiate sexual action without prompting from a male is not only unnatural but physically unhealthy.

Women involved in overt lesbian relationships were deeply underground. Records of male homosexual behaviour – the cruising grounds, clubs and networks – are available as early as the eighteenth century. There is so much less information on lesbian social identity and how it might have functioned. We know that silence was paramount, that any lesbian activity around the women's movement would have to have been secret as the grave in order to avoid adding even more controversy to their activities. The question of whether women even thought of certain activities as 'lesbian' must constantly be asked. Fooling around in bed with long nightdresses and a hot water bottle might have been seen as totally acceptable. Still, the question of deviancy hovered over the suffragettes. It was used as a way to attack their beliefs, as if only deviant women would protest their situation. Again, we feel the modern echoes – surely only badly dressed lesbians would cause a fuss over women's issues.

Under the passionate-friendships model, spinsters could live together their whole lives as friends without stigma. But when scientists began to analyze and codify lesbian behaviour and link lesbianism with the rise of women's independence, deep friendships between women became suspect. Whatever percentage of the friendships was 'innocent' and whatever was sexually active, now both were tarred with the same brush.

DOCTORS AND SEXUALITY

Victorians had a fundamental confidence in science, so physicians appeared to hold absolute truths about the nature of women. They were instrumental in defining women solely by their sexual organs and continued to reinforce the idea of the private sphere, which meant no woman was fit to become a doctor. The medical establishment came up with a number of interesting theories to support this, among them that menstruation made women incapable of any intellectual activity and that infertility arose from too much thinking.

Dr. Henry Maudsley, a respected British psychiatrist, believed that women 'by virtue of their reproductive functions, could not stand up to the rigors of higher education or sustained cerebral activity ... [N]ature had endowed women with a finite amount of energy, and its proper use belonged to reproduction ... If women foolishly attempted to undetake study ... they risked ruining forever their child-bearing capacities, thus endangering the future of the race.'[15]

In many cases, the insult to women went beyond the intellectual to the physical. Feminists charged that physicians used obstetrical examination as a cover for sexual abuse and the speculum as an instrument of torture. Abuses were legion. If women are afraid to speak of abuse now, imagine a Victorian virgin silently suffering brutal use of the speculum, enduring an examination in which the doctor uses her submission for his sexual gratification. Feminists called the attitude of doctors towards women's sexual organs violent and degrading. More than this, it was as if the male doctors created a monopoly over women's minds as well, their own common sense often submitting to the doctor's supposed knowledge. Women were staggeringly ignorant about their reproductive systems.

The line between a painful, insensitive examination and actual violation was often impossible to prove. Women rarely spoke up about enduring genital procedures which seemed completely unnecessary. A report at the time concluded that 'many women in their weakness and ignorance, are persuaded or commanded into these examinations when not the slightest *necessity* exists.'[16]

Doctors were regularly complicit with husbands in concealing venereal disease – famously rampant in the Victorian Age. They were accused of helping their male patients to camouflage gonorrheal discharge so that they could continue to have sex with their wives. Women were often ill without knowing that their husbands had communicated the disease to them, or that the disease could be passed on to their children.

But there was worse than this. The practice of performing clitoridectomies on both married and unmarried women was common in Europe until the First World War and beyond. We now consider this practice an abomination, but it's good to remember that not so long ago, it was going on in Britain as a cure for 'excessive nerves'. The case of Dr. Isaac Brown became a rallying point. In 1867, when the Obstetrical Society expelled Brown for performing clitoridectomies, his crime wasn't that he performed the operation as such, but that it had been done on married women without the knowledge or consent of their husbands. A lesser problem seemed to be that it was done without the knowledge of the women themselves, some of them unmarried. Women woke up from the operation and found the only organ in the human body with no function other than pleasure had been sawed off.

Feminists argued that female doctors would put an end to the worst abuses and that women would feel more comfortable speaking about their 'female complaints.' The medical establishment was hostile to the idea of admitting women but, in this as in other arenas, women inspired each other on both sides of the ocean. Elizabeth Blackwell became the first female doctor in America. After being rejected by twenty-two schools, she finally received her degree in Geneva in 1847. Twenty thousand people turned up to watch her graduate.

Later, Britain's Elizabeth Garrett studied by first becoming a nurse, then attending lectures meant only for doctors. Garrett discovered that the Society of Apothecaries didn't specify that females were banned from taking examinations. She took the exams and passed. As soon as Garrett was granted her certificate, the society changed its regulations to stop other women from entering the profession. In 1871, the University of Edinburgh allowed seven women to study medicine. One of them was followed in the streets by her fellow male students who shouted at her 'all the foulest epithets in their voluminous vocabulary of abuse ... using medical terms to make the disgusting purport of their language more intelligible to me.'[17]

Much of the information about women's handling by doctors came out as a result of the campaign against the Contagious Diseases Acts of 1864, 1866 and 1869, which galvanized women's rage against the medical profession. The intent of these new laws was to contain venereal disease by forcibly examining suspected prostitutes – but not their male clients. But the campaign to repeal the acts revealed a flagrant double standard and helped to bridge the gulf between respectable women and women of the night. All had endured the specular examination – it became the great leveller. The protest allowed campaigners to open up the arena of the gynecological examination of women.

It's not hard to understand why many saw the entry of women into the medical profession as a divine crusade.

PRE-MILITANCY

Throughout 1800s, the flame of the women's movement rose and fell, catching the public imagination with a publication or issue, then falling again. But it gained strength over time. This was due to countless grassroots organizations, many in the north of England, that flourished without the sexy publicity machine of the later militant period. As I read about the Yorkshire and Lancashire women's participation, I couldn't help feeling a rush of genetic pride. My father is a working-class man from Yorkshire, and I can imagine the wars that were fought with the fractious, intractable Yorkshire men and the equally obstinate Yorkshire lasses.

There's no question that I was drawn to the more sensational aspects of the women's suffrage movement. I couldn't help it – the militant period fascinated me. It was stunningly dramatic. But the creative timeline in *Age of Arousal* includes the years before the militant period as well. Even though I've reversed time in the play, I want to show what was happening before the word 'suffragette' was coined by the *Fleet Street Press* in 1906.

Especially during the pre-militant phase, from 1849 to 1906, the north of England was a hotbed, the cradle of the women's suffrage movement. In factory-worker families, the women's earnings were sometimes close to that of the men's, and while working long hours in cotton mills at the same time as they bore and cared for their children earned them a high mortality rate, it also gave them a place of power. The women's part in workers' strikes was often central, with women organizing and leading the marches while men picketed. In many instances, women were the directors of the strikes. They held the meetings, sent delegates and drew up terms. This is not to say that all was rosy in the working classes – many men resented that women were 'taking their jobs' (though wives' earnings were often a necessity), and women often received a lesser wage for the same work. Women's associations were founded to create awareness and to battle for rights both within the home and in the workplace. They fought for equal pay, child allowances and birth control, and they did it after working a full day themselves.

CLASS AND THE CAUSE

One of the main criticisms of the later militant campaign of the twentieth century was that it was mainly a middle- or upper-middle-class movement. There were working-class women involved in radical militancy, but they were not a majority. Middle-class women had the time, the education and the money to make trouble at the drop of a feathered hat. What woman would be able to spend weeks, sometimes months, in jail if she were a breadwinner? Some did manage it, somehow. There were a number of paid positions in most suffrage organizations, and these often went to members who had no private income. After being released from prison, the women were often in a desperate state of health. They were met and taken to rest houses and home hospitals where they could recover. This allowed the poorer members of the organization the same rights as the rich, at least when they were incapacitated. These houses and many other activities were funded by wealthy supporters, among them George Bernard Shaw, as well as many rich women, who donated large sums of money to keep things going. Still, whether the upper-middle-class women who headed the radical organizations did enough to allow for the participation of all classes is a valid question.

As the militant campaigns of the 1900s were gaining headlines, the constant, fundamental work of raising awareness and fighting women's poverty was done by unpaid working women. *Age of Arousal*, like Gissing's *The Odd Women*, concentrates on the dilemma of middle-class women. But this true bedrock must be acknowledged.

CONTAGIOUS DISEASES

It was the campaign to repeal the Contagious Diseases Acts of 1864, 1866 and 1869 that finally radicalized the pre-suffragette movement. The acts were established to combat the epidemic of venereal disease, or the Great Scourge, by empowering police to arrest any women suspected of being a prostitute and compelling her to submit to an examination by the dreaded speculum. Prostitutes were penalized but not their clients, who were spreading disease to the other side of the marital bed, to their pure, passionless wives and innocent children. The double standard had never been so clear, and fighting to repeal the acts brought 'good' women in contact with their sexual sisters. This battle, headed by crusading author and activist Josephine Butler, created the base for the later suffrage movement, propelling thousands of well-bred, complacent women into an activism that they never could have anticipated. There was a groundswell of anger at women's treatment at the hands of the medical establishment as well as at their status as sexual objects. The subjects of sex and prostitution had been unmentionable, but now they were out in the open.

The women who protested the acts were at first surprised by the outpouring of insult and hatred they received. It was as if, by broaching the subject of prostitution, they became prostitutes themselves, open to the foulest of insults. These ladies were suddenly hearing epithets hurled at them with a violence that was truly educating. The eminently respectable Butler, known as an outstanding orator, was called 'an indecent maenad, a shrieking sister, frenzied, unsexed, and utterly without shame.'[18] And that was the printable abuse. But Butler persevered, also fighting what was known as the white slave market, where a thirteen-year-old girl could be bought by a brothel for five pounds. As a result of her efforts, the age of consent was raised from thirteen to sixteen. Butler and countless others helped form the foundation for the even more militant twentieth-century suffragettes.

SUFFRAGETTES

I'd had always wanted to know more about the suffragettes. I had a vague idea of the hunger strikes, an even vaguer memory of somebody flinging herself under the king's horse – and then there was *Mary Poppins*. The current pop image of the suffragettes comes from the children's mother in the film. Played by Glynis Johns, the mother is a silly woman who neglects her children and wears a giant sign over her chest, 'Votes for Women.' She's a fool who gets all riled up for nothing.

The story of the suffragettes blew me away. They were organized, witty and dangerous. They are unique in history – the militant suffragettes were the first women in the world to make a policy of breaking the law and going to jail for a feminist cause. Author Gretchen Wilson, whose aunt was in the thick of the struggle, writes that, 'Never before or since has there been such a focused, forceful movement by women seeking equality with men.'[19]

At the turn of the century, the women's suffrage movement was all but dead. Northern England was the exception, with its strong participation in women's groups, but apart from this, it was hard to get twenty people to a suffrage meeting. There had been great gaps in the impetus for political action. In 1902, Christabel Pankhurst attended a talk by American suffrage pioneer Susan B. Anthony, who had been part of a protest where hundreds of American women flaunted the law by voting in a presidential election. Anthony was the only one arrested – she refused to pay the fine but was never imprisoned. This had occurred in 1872. Thirty years later, little had changed. How long could women wait to become citizens? Pankhurst began thinking of escalating the peaceful marches and protests of the past into new territory. Suffragists were about to become criminals.

Christabel's soon-to-be-famous mother, Mrs. Emmeline Pankhurst, widow and socialist, formed the Women's Suffrage Political Union (WSPU) in 1903. The new association was supposed to be all female but ended up including a few men, including Richard Pethick-Lawrence, married to Emmeline Pethick-Lawrence, and James Kier Hardie, the leader of the Independent Labour Party. The goal was to revitalize the suffrage movement and to get the right to vote.

In London at this point there were a few dreary, polite rituals around women's suffrage, which involved private meetings with MPs, the consumption of tea and crumpets and conversation aimed at getting a commitment to put forward bills to include women's rights. At one such meeting, Mrs. Pankhurst had had enough. She burst out, speaking loudly, demanding a firm assurance that the member would put forward a bill. There was much consternation about her tactics. They were rude.

More rudeness followed, as a campaign of civil disobedience began, headed by the wspu and supported by other organizations, both in London and throughout Britian. Initially, there were rallies, countless meetings and marches, including a certain amount of civil disobedience. These moments came at first spontaneously, out of pure frustration, often after the defeat of yet another proposed bill that had no chance of being passed. And, suddenly, a little old Victorian lady in ringlets is standing on the plinth of a statue giving a speech outside Westminster Abbey, the police try to stop her, someone intervenes on her behalf, the speech continues, a larger crowd gathers, they begin to march ...

Then Christabel Pankhurst and Annie Kenney, the wspu's 'factory girl and a trade unionist' and Christabel's right-hand woman, unfurl a forbidden banner at a Liberal political meeting, 'Votes for Women.' Annie Kenney rises to speak for the women of the cotton mills, and there is laughter and derision. She refuses to sit down, a constable detains her, and she and Christabel are dragged from the meeting. They are thrown into the street, where some of the audience joins them for a protest meeting. They're arrested. They secretly want to be arrested. They refuse to pay the fine and are imprisoned, Annie for three days, Christabel for seven because she spits on a policeman to make sure she gets arrested. Later she says it wasn't real spit, just a 'pursing of the lips.' However much spittle was involved, it's the very first time women are imprisoned for the cause of suffrage, and the press carries long articles. The public is interested. Suddenly, 'votes for women' is news. When Annie Kenney is released, a crowd of 2,000 gathers at the prison gates to cheer for her.

PEACE AND WAR

By 1906, suffragettes were thriving on publicity and constantly scheming to gain the attention of the press. The Ladies Gallery of the Houses of Parliament had an iron grill that separated women from the House itself. Repeatedly, women chained themselves to the grill, at one point in such a way that it had to be hack-sawed off in order to release them. It was never replaced. On many occasions, the charade of introducing a suffrage amendment created a ruckus. MPs would pretend to debate while indulging in ridicule and sarcasm, then the resolution would be voted down. Women would shout, heckle, stand on chairs, boo, sing songs and encourage crowds to stand outside the parliament buildings in protest. The police would bodily remove those inciting the demonstrations, starting scrums that became more and more violent. Increasing numbers of women came forward to be arrested for abusive behaviour and breach of the peace. The sentences became ridiculously harsh – two months in jail. Two months with the rats. The prisons, predictably, had a class system: political prisoners were housed in the 'first division', with more decent food and better conditions, while common criminals had a different experience entirely in the rat- and louse-infested second division. These ladies were sentenced as common criminals. The public was incensed. The membership of the WSPU tripled, quadrupled. By 1908, the circulation of the suffrage paper, *Votes for Women* had shot up from 2,000 to 10,000 copies a week.

The sheer numbers the movement was now able to call on were staggering. In a final effort to show Prime Minister Asquith the strength of their support, the WSPU put their money and resources into organizing one giant peaceful march to Hyde Park. The planning was meticulous. Thousands of suffragettes from all over England, from hundreds of societies and organizations, arrived in London. Informed by posters, bills and word of mouth, the public crowded London streets to see the spectacle – suffragette marches were intended to be dramatic, involving both visual and theatre artists. On a fine June day in 1908, 30,000 marchers joined together to form a procession five abreast and seven miles long. James Kier Hardie, George Bernard Shaw, Mrs. Thomas Hardy, Mrs. H. G. Wells and other notables rode in open carriages filled with garlands of flowers. Thirty thousand women walked in flowing white dresses, carrying elaborate painted banners, wearing ribbons, badges, scarves, ties and belts with the suffragette colours – purple, green and white. They walked proudly, sang lustily, heads held high. The motto was 'Deeds not Words.' The populace joined them, walking beside and behind the procession. The sun sparkled, the leaves were green, there was hope in the air. The *Times* estimated that up to half a million watchers or supporters turned out.

Nothing changed. Asquith remained immovable. The largest peaceful demonstration it had been possible to arrange had failed. Frustration became rage. A couple of young women carried out a spontaneous act that would set the stage for the next several years. Mary Leigh and Edith New placed stones in a bag, took a taxi to 10 Downing Street, and hurled them at Asquith's windows, breaking two of them. As Gretchen Wilson notes, 'Never before had women so deliberately and symbolically used violence to shout, "We no longer accept your laws."'[20] The WSPU supported the act. Militancy entered a new phase. The violence at protests escalated, the police continued to rough up marchers, sometimes brutally dislocating joints and breaking bones as they formed cordons to keep demonstrators from reaching the House of Commons. Larger numbers of protesters were ending up in hospital or prison.

In 1909, another spontaneous act cranked up the pressure. Again, it was not the WSPU leadership but the everyday members who initiated the truly creative acts of militancy. A sculptor and writer, Marion Wallace Dunlop, was sentenced to a month in Holloway Prison. She demanded to be treated as a political prisoner but was denied. In protest, she simply refused to eat. As with the stone throwing, the WSPU leaders were at first surprised, then totally supported the initiative. Within a month, everyone was doing it. The hunger strike became common practice among convicted suffragettes. It was never mandatory, but the hunger strikers became heroes, and the knowledge they were starving in bleak prison cells pushed the cause to even more extreme acts of militancy. At first, the hunger strikers confused the prison system and the women were released after forty-eight hours. A few months later, the force-feedings began.

With the force-feeding, a level of torture was achieved that destroyed many women's health for the rest of their lives. No one ever died in prison – the authorities made certain of that by releasing women on the verge of death, but there were fatalities as a direct result. Sometimes the fluid poured down ended up in the lungs, causing pneumonia. The process broke immune systems and created heart murmurs, punctured organs and ruptured digestive systems. There were two methods: in one, the feeding tube was inserted through the mouth, the other involved a tube pushed through the nasal passages. The accounts of this experience are horrific. The strain of the force-feeding could rupture veins in the eyes. The women were often let go in a few days out of fear they wouldn't survive. This meant they rarely served their full sentences, which made the government look impotent. In order to make certain that sentences were served, the 'Cat and Mouse Act' was put into effect, in which women on the verge of death were released in order to recover and then rearrested. This meant that the total amount of time served could stretch into many months. It was a new kind of torture, in which women who had barely recovered from the last set of force-feedings would undergo another series, nearly die, be released, recover, be arrested again. They went into hiding, becoming mice to avoid being caught by the law enforcement 'cat'.

The following diary entry by Gladys Roberts, a hunger striker, shows a strange pattern – no matter how committed they were or how severe the suffering, it never seemed enough. Each woman would look at another, saying, 'She is giving more'. Many thought of themselves as cowards when common sense would suggest the opposite.

> Wednesday July 14 … They have brought us a pint of cocoa and a lump of the usual bread. Hunger strike commences … Thursday July 15 … I lie on the bed – I feel so weak – breakfast has just been put in. I said I didn't want any. God help me! I wonder if those outside are thinking about us. I am a coward …[21]

If there was one incident that helped to bring on a new level of warfare, it was what came to be called 'Black Friday'. In 1910, as 300 people marched to the House after being refused a meeting with Asquith, the police assaulted the demonstrators before making arrests – they simply circled the demonstrators and began beating them. Later, the women charged that the violence was sexual in nature, that police literally tore the clothes from their bodies, yanked hair out by the handful and, in a new tactic, beat women on the breasts, or grabbed and twisted their nipples, jeering that the women 'wanted it.' The police later said that they had permission from their superiors to sexually assault the suffragettes. During the fray, it was reported that women were dragged up side streets and 'assaulted.' Some were just thrown down on the ground and kicked. It went on for hours. Mrs. Pankhurst's sister died from a heart attack a day after the event. Fifty women were laid up with injuries, 119 were arrested. Witnesses came forward to give an account of the disgrace. To avoid an inquiry, all charges were dismissed the next day.

MEN AND THE CAUSE

As always, a minority of good men stood up to be counted around the contentious issue of women's suffrage. Although most organizations were open only to women, Victorian men marched and risked their careers to support women's suffrage. Secretly, many more sympathized, though to admit it would be to lose their balls. Notwithstanding the actions of the police on Black Friday, on occasion even London bobbies found a way to lend a hand. Nearly every history of the movement includes an account of a timid suffragette attempting to get arrested for slapping policeman keeping her from entering the House of Commons. When the trembling suffragette raises her gloved hand, a bobby says cheerfully, 'Good enough, miss, now let's get you off to prison.'

There were suffrage couples throughout the world forming a united front. The husbands dedicated themselves to the cause and endured separation and enormous anxiety as their wives were jailed, force-fed or beaten during demonstrations. Although there was horrible friction in many marriages over the wife's participation in the movement, there are also inspiring examples of activist teamwork. We can only imagine what they said to Josephine

Butler's husband, George, for allowing his wife to go on the road to speak of sex, prostitution and gonorrhea.

We'll never know what went on in those bedrooms or how hard it got.

ORGANIZATION AND ESCALATION

The size and level of organization and the complex nature of the fight amazed me. By the time the post-millennial suffragettes began getting arrested, the protests and actions were run like military operations. There were many splinter groups once the violence began, but the WSPU encouraged it all. It had a paid staff, a strict hierarchy and an incredible ability to create newsworthy, attention-grabbing events. The women who worked in the WSPU and other organizations were brilliant, dedicated and witty. You can imagine them sprawled around offices, eating buns, drinking tea, planning, scheming, raising money, writing speeches, petitions and newsletters, laughing like hyenas. There is a mischievousness to what they did, especially before they were worn down by starvation, force-feeding, beatings and, worse than all of this, the betrayal of the politicians who again and again promised to support them. Suffragettes continued to storm the parliament buildings in countless ways. There were polite delegations of fifteen or so, armed with signatures and petitions, seeking to meet with Gladstone or later Asquith to put forward their case. There were demonstrations of over 3,000, which became increasingly violent. Individual women managed to sneak into the inner sanctum of the House of Commons and hang a single banner before being arrested or dragged away. As the struggle gained momentum, the mottos on banners became more forceful, finally reading 'Death or Victory.' There were multiple fronts – a peaceful decoy demonstration outside Parliament to draw the police, while suffragettes inside Westminster in the Ladies Gallery would be chaining themselves to the grill, as hundreds threw stones and destroyed property in other parts of London. All this was publicized by the suffragettes' version of a blog – *Votes for Women*, the weekly newspaper that gave updates, articles and calls to action for various campaigns. Women of all classes stood for hours in the rain and cold, selling the paper, keeping this lifeline to the organization going. The writing and theory were exemplary. In 1912, when the call to a new level of militancy began, this is how Mrs. Pankhurst put it:

> The only recklessness the Suffragettes have ever shown has been about their own lives and not about the lives of others. It has never been, and it will never be, the policy of the WSPU recklessly to endanger human life. We leave that to the enemy. We leave that to men in their warfare. No, even from the point of view of policy, militancy affecting the security of human life would be out of place. There is something that the governments care far more for than human life and that is the security of property and so it is through property that we shall strike the enemy.[22]

Breaking the law was not a first resort or even a second, but when it finally happened it came in a torrent. Ladies stood before shop windows in the West End with large stones in their hands, took a deep breath and pitched. Later, driven to greater violence, they committed arson, burning buildings to the ground while always ensuring that no one was inside. Empty mansions, houses and warehouses burned, fires raged all over the country, bombs were planted and acid was poured into mailboxes. Large-scale window-smashing campaigns continued, devastating whole streets. During these years the campaign moved from civil disobedience to property destruction on a significant scale. Not a week went by without public action. Unique in the history of violent struggle, no one was ever seriously injured during the three solid years of this level of militancy. Mrs. Pankhurst pledged 'not a cat or a canary is to be killed.' And none were. 'The WSPU arson campaign was a controlled attack, a brand of warfare unique to the female organization.'[23] They set the bar for hundreds of other suffragist groups around the world.

THE SPLIT OVER MILITANCY

But at the time, no one knew that the remarkable goal of safety within violence would be achieved. A split in the movement now occurred, one that is part of every revolutionary struggle – between those who embrace violent protest and those who do not. Although the leadership of the WSPU acknowledged that this level of militancy was not right or necessary for all, they continued to encourage it, losing many members who found these tactics unnecessary and even dangerous to the cause itself. Among those who left were the Pethick-Lawrences, central to the WSPU since the beginning. Fred Lawrence and Emmeline Pethick split from the organization in 1912, causing confusion in the ranks, but continued to fund and run the *Votes for Women* newsletter. The WSPU started its own, *The Suffragette*. Pethick-Lawrence, once the second-most prominent woman in the WSPU, became a leader in a new organization, the United Suffragists, which repudiated Pankhurstian extremes. She and many others believed that militancy was destined to escalate 'Because one cannot say of militancy "We will only go so far."'[24] *Punch* magazine divided the two groups into the Panks and the Peths.

This stage of protest was a move from martyrdom – an inward state where violence was accepted only as it would injure themselves – to an outward fist into the world of overt destruction. Some felt these activities merely copied male behaviour and lost the cause its high moral ground. They would became second-rate men as opposed to heroic women.

The call to violence reduced the fantastic numbers the movement had been able to marshal in its support. Real fear was in the air. While Mrs. Pankhurst ordered no human or animal be harmed, there were reports of women at the shooting ranges, and rumours that Asquith would be assassinated. The rumours gained some credibility when in 1913 Mary Leigh threw a hatchet into Asquith's carriage in Dublin. It might be only a matter of time before a fatality occurred, and where would this place the women who had sacrificed so much? As Annie Besant, a loyal suffragette put it, 'Once crime is entered on it must either become more and more violent until it ends in a revolution, successful or unsuccessful, or it must rouse society against the movement it claims to support, and lead to its suppression.'[25] The violent would be ousted by the more violent and, in contests like that, the most violent leads.

Some felt that the discourse around women's rights became lost in a blaze of debate over strategy. The issues became confused. An appeal to violence, even against the great god of property, was bound to be more than controversial. The subject dominated the *Suffragette*'s editorials. Critics felt the policy had the capacity to dictate debate and narrow the arguments.

Now the gloves were off. Women's rage was turning them into the maenads they had long been accused of being. They were dangerous. They could kill you by accident. They burnt letters and postcards by the thousands. It went on for three years. Those who were caught in the cat-and-mouse act were enduring the most extreme pain and disability. When Emmeline Pethick-Lawrence was screaming in her cell, violently resisting those trying to force-feed her, she held off nine wardresses in a state of enormous strength and frenzy. Mrs. Pankhurst was sentenced to three years' penal servitude, but was released weeks later, almost dead from her third hunger strike in just seventy-two days. The game became 'Can you find her to rearrest her?'

The ruses and disguises became more elaborate, as now any member of the WSPU could be arrested for the policy of endorsing violence. Body doubles were deployed to spirit members from meetings where police would be present. Members were followed by detectives. The WSPU trained strong young women to protect Mrs. Pankhurst and others from being rearrested. The proud body-guards were issued small Indian clubs which they wore tied around the waist under their skirts. The clubs dangled between their legs. They were given instruction in jujitsu, practicing their moves in hidden basements, warehouses and studios. The mind boggles.

It's easy to romanticize this period, even though the violence makes me deeply uneasy. It's all right to laugh at timid ladies planning to bomb something, but to really think of it opens up a question I don't know how to answer in myself. To travel back to the suffragettes is to encounter my own young ideas about pacifism and wonder if I believe any of it any more. Maybe not. As I read, I can feel the fire rising. Given the right circumstances, I believe I would have thrown my young life into the movement – whether I would have undertaken hunger striking or arson is a big question, but the call to plunge myself into a cause has always been strong in me. Who knows how far any of us would have gone? The question reverberates through *Age of Arousal* – how far do you go?

The suffragettes never glorified militancy. Most militants felt no enthusiasm whatever for the act in itself. "'When I had to do any militancy, I nearly died with fright," a Mrs Cohen recalled, "because I *hated* anything ... whatever to do with confrontation or disturbance of any sort.""[26] You can hear her voice even now.

By the time war was declared in 1914, it seemed that violent militancy had gone the distance. For the women's movement, war may have come as a bizarre blessing. It enabled the anti-suffragists to climb down from a position which had come to be ridiculous. It enabled the battered militants to release themselves from a policy that could result only in their deaths. This may be why Mrs. Pankhurst did an apparent about-turn. She declared a ceasefire of all militant activities and called on all her followers to help defend the country. The resources of the WSPU would now go to whole-heartedly supporting the war effort. Many of the Pankhurst followers felt betrayed. Who knows how many were relieved. Six days after war was declared, all suffrage prisoners were unconditionally released.

This 'patriotic' decision was divisive, and many comrades who had stayed true to the struggle quit the WSPU. Some felt that this reversal revealed the underlying conservatism beneath the WSPU. Mrs. Pankhurst's independent daughter Sylvia fought the government, and her mother, throughout the war with her own East End Federation, agitating for better working conditions for both women and men. Some suffragettes followed orders, pulling behind the male war machine, encouraging men to sign up, but they were also encouraging the government to allow women to enter into the work force – at the same wage as the men who left it. Now that the country needed women to exit the private sphere, there was no silly debate, even though the spectre of public and private spheres and the gender definitions that created them will haunt us far into the future.

Asquith resigned and his successor, Lloyd George, now had a way to save face. In 1918, citing their tireless contribution to the war effort – but not the years of activism that preceded it – limited suffrage was finally extended to women. To the thousands of women who had fought, barfed and bled for so many years, this partial victory must have seemed a little anti-climactic.

FROM SUFFRAGE TO THE 'F' WORD

As I felt the echoes and foretellings of this struggle reverberate through time, I began to recognize the power of language to undermine political action. In the 1970s, the women's liberation movement became 'women's libbers', just as in 1906, the women's suffrage movement became 'suffragettes'. It turned out to be good handle, but it was intended to mock. 'Bluestockings' were head-strong women who dressed badly, as later 'Birkenstocked women' intimated the same thing. Now we speak of 'second-generation feminists' and their concern that younger women don't want to use the 'F' word to describe themselves. Many shrink from the present connotations of 'feminist' – narrow, fanatic, humourless, sexless. Who wouldn't shrink? The language of revolutionary change is continually subverted and confused.

At a writer's colony in Vermont, I met one of the original protesters of the Miss America pageant in Atlantic City in 1968, where the term 'bra burner' was coined. With fabulous irony, she explained that they had tried, but not succeeded, to burn a bra and other items in a metal trash can. The rubber just wouldn't light up. It seemed perfect that the single most-used identifier of women's libbers, 'bra burners', was a lie, or at least inaccurate. Their action seemed to echo the theatricality and wit of the suffragettes.

My own relationship with the women's movement seems very conflicted to me now. My younger self was saved by the times in which I lived, by the women who opened up vast new spheres in the sixties and seventies. In my twenties, I was a writer whose milieu was provocative underground theatre, but I was also an actress working in television and film. It was a schizophrenic life. Film and TV are mainly conservative mediums – I was surviving within them. Acting ability aside, I was getting work off luck, looks and a vulnerability that was both real and pretend. The first film I did with a woman director was *Passion*, directed by Patricia Rozema. At one point she asked me if I was a feminist. I said – and I can still feel how I said it, the fear, the confusion – I said, 'I wouldn't use the word.' The cock crowed three times.

I've not always been a good feminist, but every time I've cheated my own sense of self, I've been bitten in the butt. To paraphrase St. Augustine, 'Oh Lord, make me a good feminist, just not now.'

Age of Arousal was never meant to be a summing up of this research. In a way, the research became a thing of itself. Here were the contradictions, hypocrisies and bizarre scenarios of the sex war. I felt it was a good time to admit all the flaws of the struggle while still popping the champagne. We've memorialized war with 'Lest We Forget.' The struggle for women's emancipation continues in countless parallel universes. We must endow our differences with dignity and prestige. Lest we forget.

NOTES

In Scene 10 of the play, on page 79, Rhoda quotes from Germaine Greer, *The Whole Woman* (London: Doubleday, 1999), 3 ('our lives are nobler and richer ... ').

Rhoda again quotes from Greer, page 1, in Scene 12, page 97 ('We fight for more than equality ... ').

Alice quotes and paraphrases from page 233 of *The Whole Woman* in Scene 13, page 101 ('undaunted by ill treatment ... '). On page 111, Mary quotes Alice speaking one of these lines.

Notes to the Essay

1 Susan Kingsley Kent, *Sex and Suffrage in Britain, 1860–1914* (Princeton, NJ: Princeton University Press, 1987), 3.

2 Mary Wollestonecraft, *A Vindication of the Rights of Women*, ed. Miriam Brady (London: Penguin, 1992), 257–8.

3 Andrew Rosen, *Rise Up, Women! The Militant Campaign of the Women's Social and Political Union, 1903–14* (London: Routledge, 1974): 97, quoted in Gretchen Wilson, *With All Her Might: The Life of Gertrude Harding, Militant Suffragette* (New York: Holmes and Meier, 1996), 39.

4 Kent, *Sex and Suffrage*, 30.

5 Germaine Greer, *The Whole Woman* (London: Doubleday, 1999), 1.

6 Kent, *Sex and Suffrage*, 55.

7 Kent, *Sex and Suffrage*, 30.

8 Olive Katherine Parr, *Women's Emancipation* (Devon, n.d.): 9–10, quoted in Kent, *Sex and Suffrage*, 179.

9 Arabella Kenealy, *Feminism and Sex-Extinction* (London, 1920): 186, quoted in Kent, *Sex and Suffrage*, 177.

10 Elizabeth Wolstonholme Elmy to Harriet McIlquham, 13 December 1896, Elmy Collection, quoted in Kent, *Sex and Suffrage*, 93.

11 Peter Gay, *Shnitzler's Century: The Making of Middle Class Culture 1815–1914* (New York: W. W. Norton & Co., 2003), xxiv.

12 Sheila Jeffreys, *The Spinster and Her Enemies: Feminism and Sexuality, 1880–1930* (London: Pandora Press, 1985), 86.

13 Jeffreys, *The Spinster and her Enemies*, 87.

14 Lillian Faderman, *Surpassing the Love of Men: Romantic Friendships and Love Between Women from the Renaissance to the Present* (New York, 1981): 16, quoted in Kent, *Sex and Suffrage*, 51.

15 Kent, *Sex and Suffrage*, 43.

16 J. J. Garth Wilkinson, *The Forcible Introspection of Women for the Army and Navy by the Oligarchy* (London, 1870): 26, quoted in Kent, *Sex and Suffrage*, 125.

17 Edythe Lutzker, *Medical Education for Women in Great Britain* (master's thesis, Columbia University, 1959): 26–27, quoted in Kingsley Kent, *Sex and Suffrage*, 126.

18 Kent, *Sex and Suffrage*, 10.

19 Gretchen Wilson, *With All Her Might: The Life of Gertrude Harding, Militant Suffragette* (New York: Holmes and Meier Publishers, 1996), 22.

20 Wilson, *With All Her Might*, 41.

21 Wilson, *With All Her Might*, 49.

22 Antonia Raeburn, *Militant Suffragettes* (London: New English Library, 1973), 199.

23 Wilson, *With All Her Might*, 133.

24 Brian Harrison, *Peaceable Kingdom: Stability and Change in Modern Britain* (Oxford: Oxford University Press, 1982). http://www.leedstrinity.ac.uk/histcourse/suffrage/document/violsufa.htm

25 Harrison, *Peaceable Kingdom*.

26 Harrison, *Peaceable Kingdom*.

FURTHER READING

This is not a complete bibliography of all the research material, but it includes books that were a major influence.

THEORY, HISTORY AND FEMINISM

Kent, Susan Kingsley. *Sex and Suffrage in Britain 1860–1914.* Princeton, NJ: Princeton University Press, 1987.

Without a doubt the most brilliant of all the books I read. A main source for an understanding of feminist thought at the time and the philosophies that opposed them. Especially good on the pre-militant movements of 1860 to 1906.

Jeffreys, Sheila. *The Spinster and her Enemies: Feminism and Sexuality 1880–1930.* London: Pandora Press, 1885.

Jeffreys is a major thinker in this field, and unlocks many spinster triumphs.

Rowbotham, Sheila. *Women, Resistance and Revolution.* London: Penguin, 1972.

Good for looking at the idea of female resistance right from the impudent lasses of the Canterbury Tales.

HISTORY AND WOMEN'S SUFFRAGE

Raeburn, Antonia. *Militant Suffragettes.* London: New English Library, 1973.

A basic text – the total story of the militant period. Gives a complete historical account, full of fabulous detail and personality. Excellent for getting the full picture.

Wilson, Gretchen. *With All Her Might: The Life of Gertrude Harding, Militant Suffragette.* New York: Holmes and Meier, 1996.

Includes the clearest, most concise chronology on the scope and strength of the militant period. Also the story and diaries of Canadian Gertrude Harding, who was in the thick of the struggle. And a great account of the wrecking of delicate orchids – one of the more unusual militant acts.

Liddington, Jill and Jill Norris. *One Hand Tied Behind Us: The Rise of the Women's Suffrage Movement*. London: Virago Press, 1978.

Essential reading to understand the importance of the grassroots level of the suffrage movement based in Manchester and Lancashire generally. These are heroic struggles of another kind, without huge publicity but no less amazing for it. This is the world of the textile mills, of the relationship between unions and the women's movement.

Harrison, Brian Howard. *Peaceable Kingdom: Stability and Change in Modern Britain*. Oxford: Oxford University Press, 1982, as excerpted at http://www.leedstrinity.ac.uk/histcourse/suffrage/document/violsufa.htm

Harrison is critical of militancy but not blind to its uses – he gives an important alternate picture. His point of view is vital to seeing another perspective on the struggle.

Winslow, Barbara. *Sylvia Pankhurst: Sexual Politics and Political Activism*. New York: St. Martin's Press, 1996.

Pollard, Michael. *Emmeline Pankhurst*. Chicago: Evans Brothers, 1996.

You can't go wrong with the Pankhursts – anything about them will take you right to the militant suffragettes as well as to a most fascinating family of women.

VICTORIANS AND SEXUALITY

Gay, Peter. *Schnitzler's Century: The Making of Middle-Class Culture 1815–1914*. New York: W. W. Norton and Co., 2002.

An entry in the complexities of the Victorian mind and sexuality. All through the eyes of playwright, author and bon vivant Arthur Schnitzler.

Donoghue, Emma. *Passions Between Women: British Lesbian Culture, 1668–1801.* London: Harper Perennial, 1996.

Although this book doesn't deal with the Victorian age as such, it gives a well-researched and fascinating look at this entire world. The best I read on historical gay women.

Marcus, Steven. *The Other Victorians: A Study of Sexuality and Pornography in Mid-Nineteenth-Century England.* London: Weidenfeld and Nicolson, 1966.

A mind-boggling look at Victorian perversities.

Anonymous. *The Lustful Turk.* Hertfordshire: Wordsworth Editions, 1997.

The title is the best part, but it is genuine Victorian erotica and still has the capacity to shock.

TYPE MACHINES

Bliven Jr., Bruce. *The Wonderful Writing Machine.* New York: Random House, 1954.

Pictures and stories of the beginnings of the type machine and the huge interest it created.

MODERN THEORY

Greer, Germaine. *The Whole Woman.* London: Doubleday, 1999.

Friedan, Betty. *Beyond Gender: The New Politics of Work and Family.* Washington DC: The Woodrow Wilson Center Press, 1997.

This is Friedan's new thinking and echoes Sylvia Pankhurst's beliefs in 1914.

Cohen, Marcia. *The Sisterhood: The True Story of the Women Who Changed the World*. New York: Simon and Shuster, 1988.

For those who never took Modern Feminism 101 – excellent basic look at these women.

Grant, Linda. *Sexing the Millennium: Women and the Sexual Revolution*. New York: Grove Press, 1994.

Heidenry, John. *What Wild Ecstasy: The Rise and Fall of the Sexual Revolution*. New York: Simon and Schuster, 1997.

Interesting to look at for the character of Monica and all she stands for.

NOVELS AND PLAYS

Gissing, George. *The Odd Women*. 1893, edited by Gail Godwin, Rev. Edition, Salem Press, 1974, New York

Colmore, Gertrude. *Suffragettes: A Story of Three Women*. London: Pandora Press, 1984. (First published in 1911 as *Suffragette Sally*.)

Trotter, Janet Macleod. *The Suffragette*. London: Headline Book Publishing, 1996.

Hamilton, Cicely. *Diana of Dobson's*. eds. Diane F. Gillespie and Doryjane Birrer. Calgary: Broadview Press, 2003.

Waters. Sarah. *Fingersmith*. London: Riverhead Books, 2002.

Waters, Sarah. *Tipping the Velvet*. New York: Riverhead Books, 1999.

ACKNOWLEDGEMENTS

When playwright, actor, filmmaker, director Karen Hines came to this project in the role of dramaturge three years ago, I was blessed with a fellow artist who instantly had a DNA connection to the script. Her brilliant first production met the text like a playwright's wet dream, but it is in her capacity as dramaturge that she made her greatest contribution. Her understanding of structure, her rigour with the thoughtspeak, her beautifully excruciating attention to each word, helped to hone a challenging script. She worked in careful stages, using an intellect that never got in the way of the torrid emotions of the play. Hines isn't afraid of those emotions – she can match them with her brain. She used a credo that many dramaturges could learn from: 'First, do no harm.' Her contribution was a gift central to the development of this play.

The playwright acknowledges the assistance of the 2005 Banff Playwright's colony. Duchess Productions developed *Age of Arousal* with the help of the Canada Council, the Ontario Arts Council, Playwright's Workshop Montreal, the Laidlaw Foundation and the Shaw Festival.

Duchess would like to acknowledge the following artists engaged in the previous development of this script: Marcel Bouchard, Kira Bradley, Janet Burke, Martha Burns, Leah Cherniak, Paula Costain, Philippa Domville, Sadie Evans, Onalea Gilbertson, Donna Goodhand, Nicky Guadagni, Tanja Jacobs, Chapelle Jaffe, Cary Lawrence, Elana McMurtry, Ruth Madoc-Jones, Jackie Maxwell, Laura Parken, Margaret Preston, Rick Roberts, Tara Rosling, Elizabeth Shepherd, Adrienne Smook, Jane Spidell, Waneta Storms, Kelly Thornton.

Special thanks to Kevin Kennedy, Maureen Jennings, Sarah Warren, Susan Sinclair, Tara Detwiler, Anne Braund, Michelle D'Alessandro Hatt, Jill Kelner, The Humphrey Group, Beverly Deutsch.

ABOUT THE AUTHOR

As playwright and actor, Linda Griffiths is the winner of five Dora Mavor Moore awards, a Gemini award, two Chalmers awards, the Quizanne International Festival Award for *Jessica* and Los Angeles' AGA Award for her performance in John Sayles' film *Liana*. She has twice been nominated for the Governor General's Award (*The Darling Family*, 1992; *Alien Creature*, 2000). *The Darling Family* was made into a feature film, directed by Alan Zweig. She is best known for writing (in collaboration with Paul Thompson) and performing a triple role in the play *Maggie & Pierre*, in which she played Pierre Trudeau, Margaret Trudeau and a journalist named Henry. *Maggie & Pierre* toured Canada, played the Royal Alexandra Theatre and off-Broadway. Since then, she has continued to create and perform unique, highly theatrical plays that are surreal, literate and popular. Her plays include *Alien Creature: a visitation from Gwendolyn MacEwen*, *The Darling Family* and *The Duchess: a.k.a. Wallis Simpson*. As co-authors of *The Book of Jessica*, Griffiths and native author and activist Maria Campbell created a new hybrid of theatre book, which included the play *Jessica* as well as the personal and political process of its creation. Griffiths has created collective work (*Paper Wheat, Les Maudits Anglais*), published short stories ('The Speed Christmas, 'Spiral Woman') and continues to act in theatre, television and film. In 1997, she formed her own company, Duchess Productions, which produced a tour of *Alien Creature*, as well as developing and associate-producing *The Duchess, Alien Creature, Chronic* and *Age of Arousal*. Duchess also produces Griffiths's original studio class, Visceral Playwriting. She is an Adjunct Professor to the University of Toronto's Master's Program in Creative Writing. New projects include two one-person shows, *Baby Finger* and *The Last Dog of War*.

Typeset in Sabon Next and Egyptian Slate
Printed and bound at the Coach House on bpNichol Lane, 2007.

Edited and designed by Alana Wilcox
Cover image by Matt Saunders

Coach House Books
401 Huron Street on bpNichol Lane
Toronto, Ontario M5S 2G5

416 979 2217
800 367 6360

mail@chbooks.com
www.chbooks.com